BASEMENTS
How to

Real People – Real Projects®

HOMETIME®

Publisher: Dean Johnson
Editor: Pamela S. Price
Writers: John Kelsey, Laura Tringali
Art Director: Bill Nelson
Associate Editor: Jason Adair
Copy Editor: Lisa Wagner

Hometime Hosts: Dean Johnson, Robin Hartl
Project Producers: Matt Dolph, Wade Barry
Construction and Technical Review: Chris Balamut,
Mark Kimball, Dan Laabs, Judd Nelson
Production Crew: Tom (Buki) Weckwerth, Mark
Gutzmer, Scott Burdick

Illustrator: Mario Ferro
Photographer: Jeff Lyman
Cover Photo: Maki Strunc Photography
Electronic Imaging: Jennifer S. Parks

Production Coordinator: Pam Scheunemann
Electronic Layout: M. Elizabeth Salzmann

Book Creative Direction, Design, and Production:
MacLean & Tuminelly, Minneapolis, MN
Cover Design: Richard Scales Advertising Associates

Electronic Prepress: Encore Color Group
Printed by: RR Donnelley & Sons Co.
Printed in the United States

5 4 3 2 / 03 02

Library of Congress Catalog Card Number 97-74100
ISBN 1-890257-03-6

H O M E T I M E®
4275 Norex Drive
Chaska, MN 55318

Special Thanks: ALA's Health House; Mike
Tambornino, Architectural Sales of Minnesota;
Armstrong World Industries; Bill Evans, Jim Beck,
B.E. Mechanical; City of Chanhassen Building
Officials; Congoleum Corp.; Custom Wine Cellars &
Racks; Heating & Cooling Two; Mike 'Goose' Alden,
Jerry's Floor Store; Jim Johnson; KraftMaid
Cabinetry, Inc.; NuTone; Owens Corning; Peter's
Billiard Supply; Rite-Way Waterproofing; Sunburst
Heating & Air; Keith Terry; Tom Gestach,TJ
Replacement Windows; Bill Schmid, University of
Minnesota

Contributing Photography: Armstrong World
Industries, Bruce Hardwood Floors, John Kelsey,
Maxxon Corporation, Zoeller Pump Company,
Michael R. Evans, Saunatec, Inc.

The procedures described here are for people with
average home repair skills. If you're inexperienced
in the use of tools or equipment described, or if
you're uncertain whether the procedures discussed
are appropriate for your specific situation, consult a
skilled professional before you begin work.

Our materials and procedures are based on
common practice and the prevailing Uniform
Building Code (UBC) at the time this book was
written. Local regulations may vary from the UBC,
and the UBC may also change periodically. Always
check relevant local regulations and obtain
necessary permits before starting work. Follow all
manufacturer instructions for the use of hand and
power tools, and seek professional help if the
instructions in this book deviate from
manufacturers' use-and-care guidelines.

The authors disclaim any liability for injury or
damage resulting from the use of tools or
procedures described in the text. Proper use of
equipment and products is your responsibility, and
your performance is at your own risk.

*For online project help and information on other
Hometime products, visit us on the Web at*
www.hometime.com

Introduction

Robin Hartl

Dean Johnson

We think that finishing a basement is one of the best large-scale projects there is for a do-it-yourselfer. How else can you add that much living space without tearing the back wall off the house or raising the roof? What's more, if you do a good job of masking off the basement, there's no reason the work going on down there has to affect life in the rest of the house – except for a few hours every now and again when you have to turn off the power or the water.

Unlike remodeling kitchens or bathrooms, finishing a basement shouldn't cramp your lifestyle. Because the project won't inconvenience the family, you can work on it at your own pace. You can even take a weekend off now and then. (Did we mention that finishing a basement isn't as hard on marriages as other remodeling projects?)

Don't take too many weekends off, though. Most building permits expire after a year and we've discovered the hard way that renewing one means paying the application fee a second time.

Table of Contents

PLANNING
and DESIGN

The planning and design stage of a basement remodel is, in many ways, the most important part of the entire project. A well-thought-out plan will guide you through each step of the job and help you stay within budget. Along the road to developing a plan, you'll have to confront some critical issues. You'll have to figure out how you want to use the basement, resolve any structural issues, and decide how much of the work you realistically can do yourself. You'll also have to figure out a schedule to make sure the work progresses smoothly to completion.

Figuring Out Your Needs

Finishing off a basement is a good way to increase the living area – and the resale value – of your home at a reasonable cost. While the cash you put into improvements seldom yields a dollar-for-dollar return at resale, finished basements score high among typical upgrades. Keep in mind, though, that local market conditions will influence the resale value of any improvements. If you're planning to sell in the next few years, ask a real estate agent to help you determine what size budget makes sense for your neighborhood.

Depending on the size of the basement, you can add a bedroom, bathroom, media room, workshop, or even a home office. This is the real payback of a remodel – what the new space is worth to you, the homeowner. When planning out the space, consider headroom, lighting, and stairway access, as well as the unique construction challenges of the individual rooms. Headroom can be a real problem, especially if the ceiling is crisscrossed by ductwork or pipes. Building codes have strict headroom specifications for all rooms, typically requiring that most basement spaces have at least 90 inches of headroom over at least half the area of the room. (Bathrooms usually can have less headroom.) Lighting lower-level spaces also requires careful thought. Since natural light is often scarce in basement rooms, you will have to compensate with a good lighting design for each of the rooms.

If you'll be constructing a bedroom, your building code will require that you provide an emergency exit for escape in case of fire. This may be either a door or a window, but size requirements will be spelled out quite clearly. Adding a bathroom (which many people do when the basement will contain a bedroom) presents another challenge because new fixtures will have to be tied into existing plumbing lines.

Designing a basement media room offers a wealth of opportunities. Evaluate the needs and interests of everyone who will be using the room, and plan the space accordingly. Build in extra electrical outlets to handle everything from fitness machines to video games; likewise, additional cable

A basement workshop benefits from good lighting and a lot of storage space. Include a way to collect dust and plan for plenty of outlets – 240V outlets may be needed to accommodate heavy shop equipment.

In a basement wine cellar you can maintain the temperature and humidity levels required for the long-term storage of wine. If you collect wine, you should consider a temperature control system just for the wine cellar.

A game room is often used for more than one type of game – during design, it's important to allow enough space for each of the games being played. The minimum area for an 8-foot pool table, for example, should be 14 by 17 feet.

A suspended ceiling is a reasonably priced way to cover all the obstructions in a basement ceiling. While it allows access to the pipes and cables above, it does eat up headroom.

outlets and phone jacks will make the space more versatile. This is especially true if part of the space will be used as a home office, which typically has to accommodate a variety of electronic components. You'll also have to carefully plan file storage and bookshelves – built-ins free up valuable floor space.

Building a budget

Creating a wish list of all the rooms and items you'd like to incorporate into your new basement space is the fun part of the project, and it's fine to let your imagination run wild. You'll be brought back to earth soon enough.

As you finalize your plans for the basement, get prices for everything that will go into your remodel. Compile two running lists as you do your homework – one for items you wish you could have and another for those you realistically can afford. You might find that by juggling the budget a little a few of your wishes can make the final cut.

After you've determined how much you can afford to spend, reduce the budget by 10 to 20 percent. Put this money in a contingency fund to cover unexpected costs. Even the best-planned projects yield surprises which can add up to a lot of money. A contingency fund covers these expenses and ensures that you won't have to scramble for more money to finish your project.

Anything's possible in a basement remodel, as long as you do thorough planning. Shown here is a home spa that includes a sauna and a steam bath.

Newer homes often have roughed-in plumbing in the basement area. This makes adding a bathroom easier and a lot more economical than having to start from scratch.

Floor trusses are an asset in any basement remodel. They allow pipes, wires, and ductwork to be run in both directions without reducing headroom.

An egress window for a bedroom has to conform to strict code specifications to provide easy escape for you and easy access for emergency personnel.

Evaluating the Space

Before you go too far with your remodeling plans, take a hard look at the existing space. Certain aspects of your basement will be difficult or expensive to change. Once again, consider headroom. If ducts, pipes, and ceiling joists obstruct the space at every turn, it may take too much time and money to turn the basement into a livable space. Likewise, problems with radon (an odorless, colorless carcinogenic gas) must be fixed. Removing asbestos (often used in older homes around pipes and furnaces) can be expensive, but if the asbestos is in good shape and won't be disturbed during construction, you could leave it alone and contain it behind a wall or ceiling. And although hairline cracks in foundation walls are easily fixed, larger cracks in a foundation that is still settling will continue to open up after repair unless the problem is permanently solved.

By contrast, there are a variety of common conditions that fall under the heading of inconveniences rather than obstacles. Outdated plumbing, electrical, and heating and ventilating systems can all be upgraded. If it's impossible to tie into the existing heating system, independent electric baseboard heating can be installed in basement rooms, provided it won't overload the existing electrical system. Inconveniently located posts can be boxed in and turned into attractive (or at least inconspicuous) columns. Rickety stairs can be ripped out and rebuilt. Concrete slabs

Rotten wood framing members will have to be replaced during remodeling. Before you start, identify – and correct – the source of the problem.

that are in poor condition can be resurfaced, provided the conditions that caused the damage have been corrected.

Inspect all the wood in the basement, including posts, beams, and joists. If any pieces are rotted, they will need to be replaced. You may also find that some joists have sagged over time because the framing members were sized too small to begin with or they were given inadequate support. In either case, it's inexpensive to beef up the framing.

Water problems

One concern that should never be downplayed is seasonal leakage or flooding. Any money invested into a basement remodel is money down the drain if water problems aren't corrected. Fixing a damp or wet basement can be as simple as repairing gutters or as complex as digging out the foundation to waterproof the walls and install a new footing drain. Either way, it makes sense to solve your water problems before you begin remodeling.

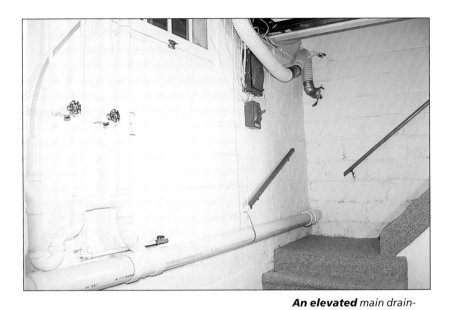

An elevated main drainpipe is a liability if you'll be adding a bathroom to the basement. You won't be able to easily tie in new plumbing and you'll need a sewage ejector to pump waste up to the drainpipe.

Basement stairs are often steep and short with insufficient headroom. They'll have to be upgraded during the remodel.

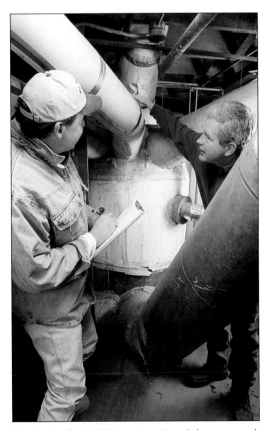

Evaluate the HVAC system. Does it have enough capacity to provide heating and cooling to the new basement rooms? Can it easily be hidden in a separate utility room? Replacing a huge old gravity system like this one will not only free up space, but will also heat the rest of the house more efficiently.

A cracked, crumbling slab can let moisture in. The source of the problem has to be identified and corrected, and you need to fix the slab before any work begins.

Designing the Space

If your house was built in the last ten years or so, chances are the original blueprint includes plans for finishing the basement. Unfortunately, that plan is probably just a standard plan and not likely to reflect your ideas for how the space should be used. For that, you'll need a new plan. You can draw your own or work with a professional.

Measure the length *of the walls all the way around the room and note the dimensions on your sketch. Mark the locations of all doors, windows, and other permanent fixtures.*

Plan the space *carefully to make sure you'll have adequate room for the equipment and furniture that you want to include. It helps to mark the placement of the walls and large pieces of furniture with masking tape or pieces of lumber.*

Drawing a floor plan

You don't need to be a skilled draftsperson or an architect to lay out and draw floor plans for your basement remodel. All you need are a few basic drawing instruments and measuring tools, such as a pencil, ruler, tape measure, and some ¼-inch-scale (¼ inch equals 1 foot) graph paper.

Begin by making a freehand sketch of your present basement floor plan that shows the layout of the walls. Next, carefully measure the lengths of the walls all the way around the room, noting the dimensions on the sketch. Then measure and mark the locations of all doors, windows, and other permanent features.

Once you've recorded these critical measurements, you're ready to make a more precise scale drawing on graph paper (or develop a plan using computer software) using your sketch as a reference.

After drawing all the walls, windows, and doors, take this basic floor plan into the basement and recheck your dimensions. All the numbers should add up. Then make copies so you can try out different ideas.

Designing the space

One of the secrets of successful design is choosing a room's focal point and designing around it. It may be a set of French doors, a fireplace, or even a pool table with a hanging

fixture above it. Designing around a focal point gives you a place to start and will help keep your design decisions on track.

Sketch out different ideas on the copies of your floor plan. Don't throw any away – you may eventually want to combine ideas from several different versions. Space-planning kits are another way to try out ideas – they provide precut plastic templates for various types of furniture pieces as well as templates for walls, windows, and doors. They're easy to work with, but you can't save your design options.

Pay extra attention to the requirements of any special items that will go into the basement, such as a sauna or pool table. If you'll be installing cabinets in a home office or media room, you can work with standard dimensions during initial design stages, but be sure to check the product specifications before finalizing the plans.

If you'll be installing a bathroom, and have existing drains for the toilet and tub/shower, try to come up with a plan that leaves them where they are. If you can make your ideas work while accommodating existing plumbing rough-ins, you'll save yourself a lot of work. When you draw the bathroom, make sure you use the exact fixture dimensions and clearances listed in the manufacturer's literature. You also need to provide a certain amount of clear space around the toilet, so check with your building department for local requirements.

The hardest part of finishing a basement is designing a space that doesn't feel like a basement. The key to this is a good lighting plan. A lighting scheme is usually broken into three components. Ambient light is the general lighting in a room. In a basement it is usually provided by recessed lights, because they don't chew up precious headroom. After you figure out your ambient lighting scheme, plan your accent and task lighting. Think

A space planning kit lets you experiment with many options. Work with the product literature so you'll be able to include the right clearances for items such as plumbing fixtures and cabinets.

Windows, wall sconces, and recessed ceiling lights provide this gameroom with so much light that it doesn't seem like a basement. Because windows with muntins are so rarely seen in a basement, they too contribute to the sense that this is a main-level room.

about items you want to highlight (art, architectural details, etc.) and areas that need task lighting (bathroom mirrors, desks, and reading chairs are a few common ones).

When planning lighting, don't automatically overlook fluorescents. Although the light cast by some fluorescents can look cooler and more artificial than light given off by incandescent bulbs, there are types of fluorescent lights that throw off a warmer light. These bulbs are rated at less than 3000 degrees K (Kelvin).

While you're planning, you should take a walk (real or imaginary) through the space and map out locations for receptacles and switches. Make sure there are receptacles for lights, entertainment equipment, computers, and hair dryers. Put light switches in logical locations that won't leave you fumbling in the dark.

Finally, when everything's laid out the way you want it, refer to the tracing paper and make an accurate, detailed plan of the way the basement will look after remodeling. Do a final check of all dimensions.

Working with a professional

If you will be dividing a large basement into several rooms, and think that you might need

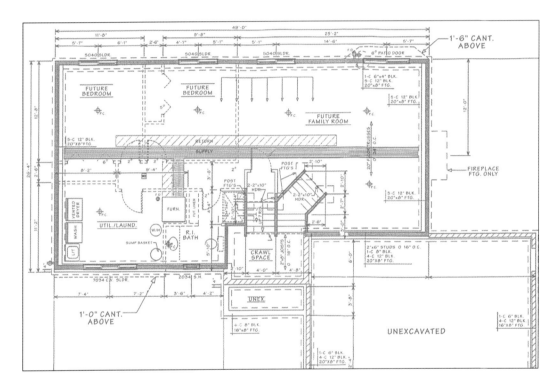

The original blueprint for your house may include plans for finishing the basement. While they may have looked just fine at the time the house was built, chances are that after a few years of living in the house you have your own ideas about how the space should be used.

 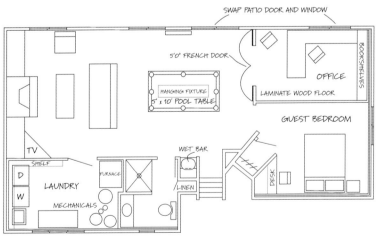

Design software allows you to create a design (right), then make variations so you can try other ideas. Other useful features include estimating tools that let you see the effect of your design choices on your budget, and 3-D software (left) that lets you view the plan from all angles. Include furniture and cabinets on the plan so you know that everything you've planned will actually fit.

extensive heating, plumbing, or electrical work, or if you're just having trouble visualizing a floor plan, you may want to enlist the help of a professional. An architect, designer, or remodeling contractor can suggest different layout options and can also draft your final working plan. Before hiring anybody, make sure to check references and take a look at their past work.

Building plans

The plans you or your designer have drawn will clearly lay out how the space will be used. Unfortunately, you can't build from them and you won't get a building permit with them. For that you need construction details added by a draftsman, architect, or builder.

This plan will include dimensions, framing details, and the size and location of all the doors and windows. Information on the mechanical systems is usually shown on separate sheets. These will show where all the electrical fixtures are located and how the circuits are wired, where the plumbing fixtures are and how they're drained and vented, and where the HVAC ducts are located.

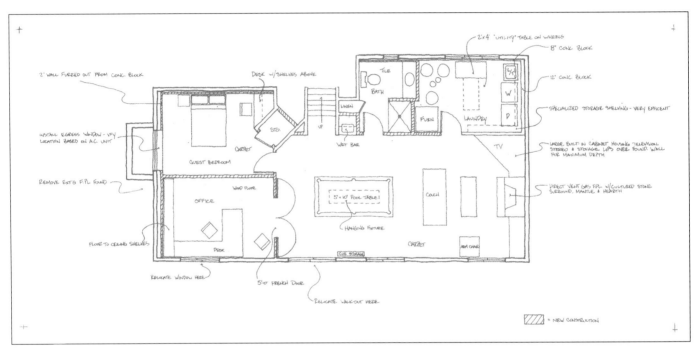

A new floor plan, drawn by you or by a designer, shows changes in the way the space will be used. Including furniture and fixtures allows you to make sure everything you want will fit and that there's good traffic flow through the rooms. While the plan is drawn to scale, it's not precise enough to build from.

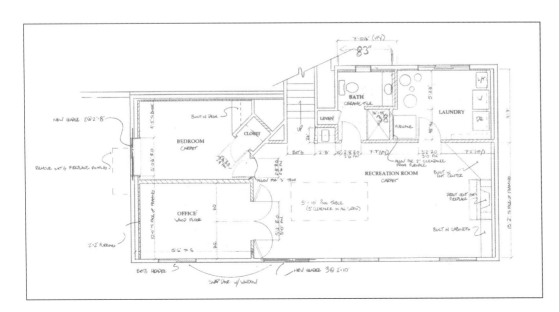

The construction plan includes precise dimensions. It shows what is existing and what is new. Additional sheets contain electrical, plumbing, and HVAC plans. Make several copies of your plans. If you plan to hire out parts of the remodeling job, give a copy to each subcontractor you ask to submit a bid. You will also have to give the building department a copy – or two – when you apply for your building permit.

Don't throw your money away

Skipping these next few pages could cost you money. Be honest – the last things you probably want to deal with (or read about) are schedules, permits, contractors, and the like. But keep in mind that there's nothing more important in a remodeling project than controlling the job, and to do that, you have to make a good construction plan and stick to it.

Construction Planning

Once you're done with your building plans, you're ready for the construction planning part of the job. Now is the time to get permits, decide which part of the work you can do yourself, and set a firm budget. You'll also have to think about where to store all those building materials you'll be ordering.

The best way to control construction costs is to do as much of the work as you can by yourself. This depends on your skill level, remodeling experience, and your spare time. Underestimating how long it will take to do a job – and overestimating your free time – are the most common mistakes you can make. Also check your local building codes to see if you're allowed to do your own plumbing and electrical work. In some areas, only licensed professionals are allowed to do this work.

Scheduling

Construction scheduling is more art than science. Use the flow chart below to plan your

The order of events

Every basement remodel is different, but the general sequence of steps doesn't change much. Skip over any steps listed here that don't pertain to your project, but try to stay in sequence. You may choose to hire out parts of the project such as the HVAC, electrical, or plumbing work. Use this timeline to make sure you bring each sub in at the appropriate time. The amount of time required for each step depends on the size and the scope of the job.

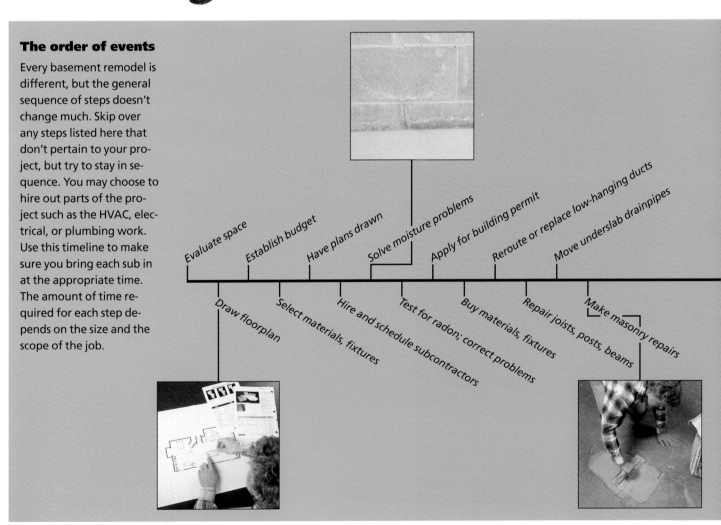

Evaluate space · Establish budget · Have plans drawn · Solve moisture problems · Apply for building permit · Reroute or replace low-hanging ducts · Move underslab drainpipes

Draw floorplan · Select materials, fixtures · Hire and schedule subcontractors · Test for radon; correct problems · Buy materials, fixtures · Repair joists, posts, beams · Make masonry repairs

job. All basement remodels follow a logical work sequence – don't skip around or you could find yourself in trouble down the line. Also, remember that obtaining a building permit is a process that can take anywhere from a few days to a few weeks. Separate permits are usually required for building, plumbing, electrical, and heating.

Hiring a Contractor

If you'll be hiring out some of the work, get itemized, written quotes from at least three licensed contractors. If the work includes providing building materials, be sure that they're specified in writing. This way you'll be able to accurately compare estimates.

Word-of-mouth is probably the best recommendation a contractor can receive – ask friends, neighbors, and architects for the names of contractors they've used and been happy with. When you've narrowed down the field, get your three written estimates with itemized labor and materials costs. Don't be tempted to take the lowest bid, because if it

seems too good to be true, it probably is. Also, insist on fixed-price bids; if you agree to pay an hourly rate, the job may never end.

Be sure that all hired help is bonded, insured, and licensed. Make sure the contractor carries valid liability and workers' compensation insurance; ask the contractor to have the insurance company send copies of the insurance certificates directly to you. In addition, check out each contractor with your local consumer affairs office, the Better Business Bureau, and local trade associations. Make sure there are no complaints on file against the contractor. Finally, control the job by controlling the money. Make lump-sum payments only for completed work, withholding 10 percent until all punch-list items are completed. Get signed lien waivers from the contractor and all subs who work on the job.

Contracts

A general contractor will probably have a standard contract – read it carefully before you sign. The contract should include start

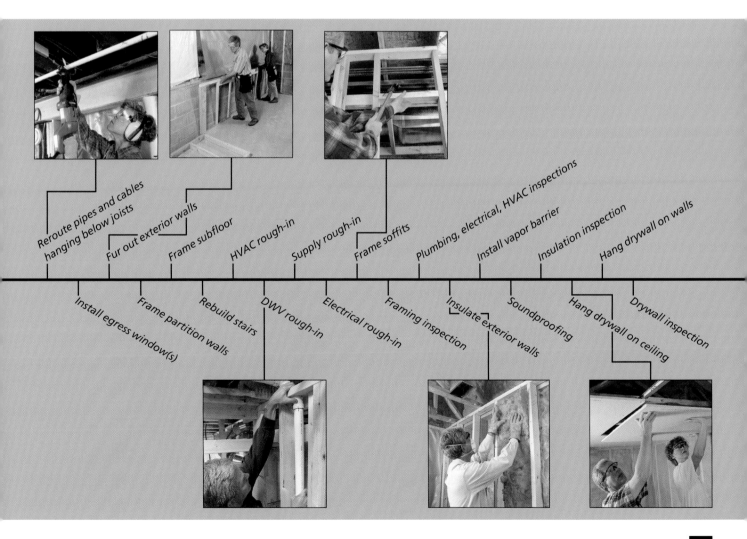

Each bid should contain an itemized list of materials and project steps. That makes it easier to compare bids and creates a better understanding between you and the contractor as to what the job will – and will not – include.

and completion dates, a payment schedule, lien waivers, and how you're going to handle change orders.

If you're working with a subcontractor (someone specializing in one particular trade) you typically both sign the bid to make it binding. When the job is complete, the sub signs a lien waiver (get the forms at a stationery store) and you write out a check to pay for the job.

Permits

Don't skip the permit process. If you get caught, and you likely will if you sell your house, you could end up paying a fine plus the cost of having everything torn out and done again. Also, for example, if illegally installed wiring causes a fire, your homeowner's insurance company might deny your claim.

The building inspector performs scheduled inspections to ensure that all work is done according to code. Ask for an inspection schedule and be sure to get required inspection sign-offs before proceeding to the next step in the project.

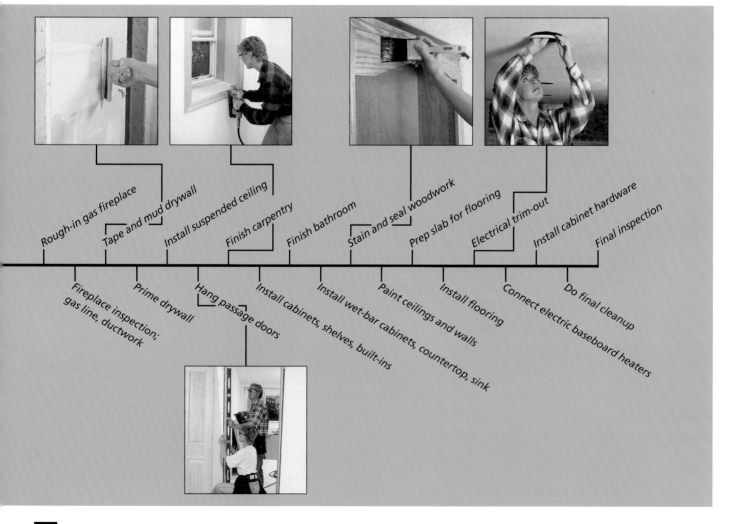

Rough-in gas fireplace

Tape and mud drywall

Install suspended ceiling

Finish carpentry

Finish bathroom

Stain and seal woodwork

Prep slab for flooring

Electrical trim-out

Install cabinet hardware

Final inspection

Fireplace inspection: gas line, ductwork

Prime drywall

Hang passage doors

Install cabinets, shelves, built-ins

Install wet-bar cabinets, countertop, sink

Paint ceilings and walls

Install flooring

Connect electric baseboard heaters

Do final cleanup

MOISTURE ISSUES

Any labor or materials *invested in finishing a basement with water problems is a waste of time and money. Moisture will rot wood, drywall, carpet, and almost any other material you might be using, as well as encourage the growth of mold and mildew. Even if there's no current leaking, signs of past water damage may indicate it's only a matter of time before water becomes a problem again.*

Many moisture problems can be remedied with simple measures and common repairs; others require a more aggressive approach. If you think you have a serious water problem, consult a licensed waterproofing contractor who has sound credentials and references. Permanent solutions can involve costly excavation in order to waterproof the outside walls of the foundation and to run a new drain along the footings.

Diagnosing the Problem

The first step in troubleshooting a wet basement is to determine whether the problem is caused by condensation or by water seepage. Condensation forms when warm moist air encounters a cool surface. Moist air can enter the basement through open windows and doors when it's humid or raining, or water vapor can be given off by damp walls. Circulating dry air, running a dehumidifier, and insulating cold-water pipes to keep them from sweating can all help to cure condensation-caused dampness in a basement.

Problems with seepage can be trickier to resolve. Water can enter the basement in a variety of ways. Typically, you'll be able to trace water problems back to faulty or missing gutters and downspouts or to an improperly pitched driveway, sidewalk, or patio that channels rain and snow runoff directly to the walls of the foundation. The grade of your property is important, too – the yard should be sloped away from the house. Landscape plantings that are too close to the foundation can trap water and moisture, which will eventually seep into the basement.

Dealing with a high water table

Although surface water around the house is the reason for most moisture problems in basements, occasionally a high water table is the culprit. (Water table is a term used to describe how deep the ground is saturated with water. The line between saturated and unsaturated soil is called the water table.) The depth of the water table will vary according to the soil, the season, and the topography of the area. After a heavy rainfall, the water table will rise, which could cause water to seep through your basement floors

Test for condensation by taping squares of heavy plastic to various parts of the floor and walls. Check back in two days. Moisture on top of the plastic comes from condensation. Moisture under the plastic is due to seepage – a more complicated problem to resolve.

Wrap cold-water pipes with foam insulation sleeves to prevent them from sweating. The sleeves are slit to snap in place over the pipes. Secure the insulation with tape or clamps, especially around elbows where the sleeves are likely to gape open.

and walls. If you regularly experience seasonal flooding, you'll probably need to take drastic measures. Begin by consulting with a licensed waterproofing contractor. You may have to put in a sump pump, tear up the perimeter of the slab to install a perimeter drain, or excavate the ground around the house down to the footings and install drain lines around the foundation.

The joint between the footing and the walls is a prime suspect when troubleshooting water problems because water can easily be pushed up through any cracks. When you see water stains and efflorescence (white crystalline patches) on basement walls, you should monitor the situation.

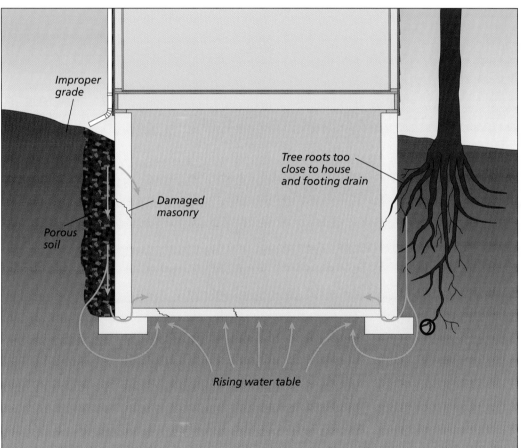

Improper grade

Porous soil

Damaged masonry

Tree roots too close to house and footing drain

Rising water table

Water entering through a basement wall is often the result of poor exterior drainage (improper grade and poorly installed gutters and downspouts being the most common culprits). Pooling water wicks through the foundation walls or leaks in through cracks or holes. The joints between concrete blocks can also allow water to leak through.

Water leaking in through the slab may indicate a problem with the joint where the walls meet the slab, a high water table, or an existing drain line that is clogged.

The roots of trees and shrubs planted too close to the foundation can hold water against the foundation and can even crack the foundation, creating a path for water to enter.

Solutions to Water Problems

There are several solutions that you can try to rid your basement of water problems. Some are simple, some require major investments of time and money. Naturally, you'll want to try the simpler solutions first.

Gutters and downspouts

A sound, correctly installed gutter system will channel roof runoff away from the foundation – it's your first defense against pooling water that could seep into your basement. Consider installing gutters if the roof overhang is less than 2 feet. Gutters come in 4- and 5-inch widths; if the roof is larger than 750 square feet, choose the wider gutter. You'll need one downspout per 35 feet of gutter. The flow of the downspout should be routed about 10 feet away from the foundation.

Clean out gutters and downspouts as needed, and at least once in the fall. Clogged gutters won't drain and the water that spills over the top may collect near the house and eventually seep in through the foundation

Check the slope of each gutter with a long level. Gutters should pitch about ¼ inch for every 4 feet. If necessary, adjust the gutters so they slope from the high end to the downspout.

Unclogging a downspout

To clear a downspout quickly and easily, snake the nozzle of a garden hose into the downspout, plug around the hose with rags, and turn on the water full force. The blast of water should dislodge debris and unblock the downspout. You can also use a plumber's snake to clear a badly clogged downspout. If both of these methods fail, you'll just have to disassemble the parts and clean them.

Attach a long downspout extension to carry water away from the foundation of the house. If you're using a short extension (minimum 2 to 4 feet), put a splash block underneath to keep soil from eroding.

Some gutters connect to an underground drain that carries water to a community storm drain. Contact your local public works department to see if there is an existing storm-water system in your area. Most utilities won't permit you to divert rainwater into the sewer line.

walls. Likewise, leaky gutters have the same effect. When you're cleaning your gutters, inspect their condition and make repairs where necessary. Also inspect the downspouts and make sure they're securely attached to the gutters.

Grading

Many basement water problems are a result of poor grading. Ideally, all surfaces should slope away from the house. A slope of 1 inch in 4 feet (a 2% grade) is the minimum for water to flow across a driveway, sidewalk, or patio. You may have to regrade, repave, or rebuild these surfaces to make them conform.

When regrading your yard, use a level and a straight 2x4 to measure grade over short distances. Over longer distances, use a line level, builder's level, laser level, or surveyor's transit. Tackle the area to be regraded with a pick and shovel; for large areas, consider calling in a landscaping contractor. Remember to divert water to your community's gutters and storm drains – not to sewers, your neighbor's yard, or your own septic system.

Where property slopes toward the house, digging a swale (a shallow trench) is a good way to carry away runoff. Dig the swale about 6 feet out from the foundation, fill it with gravel, cover it with soil, and seed it with grass seed.

Installing a drywell (a deep hole filled with gravel where a swale or underground drain can empty) usually won't solve all your water problems. Drywells eventually get clogged, and even new ones may have trouble handling a heavy downpour.

Measure grade over short distances with a level and a straight 2x4. Raise the low end of the level until the bubble indicates level, then measure the drop. If the level slides around, tape it to the 2x4.

Foundation drains and sump pumps

A perimeter drain inside the house requires cutting a trench in the concrete floor and laying in drainpipes over gravel and a membrane. If you'll be doing this work yourself, rent a jackhammer to speed the digging. The drain line usually connects to a sump pit positioned at the lowest point of the floor.

A skid loader may be required to move earth, dig trenches, and move piles of materials on a large project. While you can rent one and do the work yourself, you're probably better off hiring a contractor.

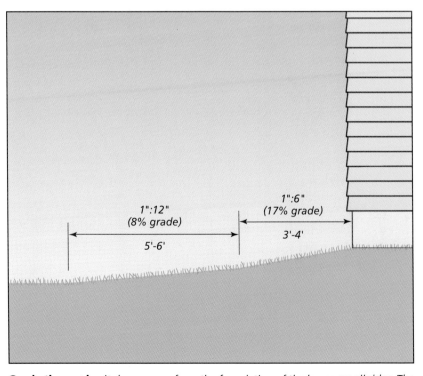

Grade the yard so it slopes away from the foundation of the house on all sides. The grade should drop 1 inch in every 6 inches near the foundation and 1 inch in 12 inches over the next 5 to 6 feet.

Water is pumped out of the pit with either a submersible or a pedestal sump pump. Water pumped out of the sump pit should be channeled out of the house and as far away as possible. Never route sump water into your floor drain, utility sink, or municipal sewage treatment system.

Installing an exterior foundation drain is a big, expensive job and usually a last resort. The idea is to dig all the dirt away from the foundation and footings, then install a drainpipe which will collect water and lead it away from the foundation. It's best to daylight the drainpipe so the water can drain into the yard or a storm sewer. If the drain can't be daylighted, it will have to be run under or through a footing so it can drain into a sump pit.

While the foundation's walls and footings are exposed, a waterproofing system is usually applied to the exterior foundation walls. There is a range of waterproofing systems available including flexible sheeting, rigid plastic drainage boards, and spray-on systems. Waterproofing technology is evolving so rapidly that your best bet is to research which systems have worked well in your area. Exterior footing drains and waterproofing are not do-it-yourself jobs – you'll want to hire an experienced contractor with good references.

A sump pit measures about 18 inches in diameter and is made from plastic or corrugated metal. Install it on top of 2 inches of gravel. Dig down deep enough so the mouth of the sump pit will be even with the basement floor. Remember to provide a nearby electrical outlet.

To daylight

Free-draining backfill

Waterproofing membrane

Footing drain

To daylight

Rigid insulation or drainboard

Discharge pipe

Interior drainpipe

6 mil poly

2" foam insulation

Sump pit

1½" rock

Two drainage options are shown here. An interior drain system drains into a sump pit, and from there out into the yard. It's a lot of hard work, but an interior drain can be installed by a D-I-Yer. Retrofitting an exterior drain system is a job for a pro. Soil is excavated from the foundation walls so that the drain can be installed along the base of the footings. Usually the foundation walls are waterproofed at the same time. The pipe should daylight and drain into the yard or a storm drain.

A submersible pump sits in the pit, which is backfilled with gravel. It connects to a discharge pipe that exits through the rim joist and routes the water as far as possible away from the house. Installation of a sump pump must meet your local building codes.

Masonry Repairs

Fill cracks as soon as you notice them – before moisture penetrates, freezes, expands, and enlarges the crack. Vinyl concrete patch works for small cracks; use pre-mixed patching mortar for large cracks. Chisel out the crack, remove loose bits of concrete with a wire brush, and clean the area with concrete cleaner. Cracks that enlarge even after they've been repaired may indicate a structural problem. In that case, call in an engineer for an evaluation.

Damp basements may benefit from a coat of waterproofing paint, but the paint won't solve a serious water problem, even if it claims to be able to withstand moderate water pressure. Still, these products help keep a basement dry. There are a variety of products available – all should be applied only after foundation walls have been cleaned and repaired. If there's efflorescence on the walls, remove it with a bristle brush and a solution of water and etching compound.

1 ***Enlarge the crack slightly*** *with a cold chisel and small sledgehammer. Hold the chisel at an angle to undercut the crack, forming a key to lock the patching material in place. When you're done, the crack should be wider at the bottom than at the top.*

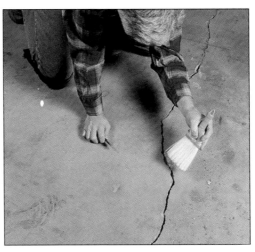

2 ***Brush all the debris out*** *of the crack. To keep cracks from opening between the patch and the surrounding concrete, apply water or bonding agent to the edges of the crack. This will keep moisture from wicking out of the patching compound into the concrete.*

3 ***Pack patching compound*** *into the crack with a pointing trowel, forcing the material down with the edges of the trowel. Smooth the patch and feather out the edges so they're flush with the surrounding concrete.*

To repair cracked mortar joints *between blocks, chisel out the cracked or loose mortar (remove about ¾ to 1 inch) and brush out any debris. Dampen the joints then pack the mortar in with a pointing trowel. Tool the joints with a jointer before the mortar sets up.*

Self-leveling floor compounds

Self-leveling products are used to fill low spots, cracks, and holes in a concrete slab. You can either buy do-it-yourself products or hire the job out. For either procedure you must first clean the slab of all dirt, grease, and old paint, fill cracks that the leveler could leak through, and then prime the slab.

The leveling products are applied in bands about a foot wide and up to ⅝" deep. The leveler begins to set quickly, so don't mix up any more than you can apply in about 15 minutes. To do the job, you'll need two people – one to mix and one to pour. Be aware that you may occasionally have to help some self-leveling products do their thing – have a float handy just in case.

Radon

Radon is a radioactive gas formed by the disintegration of uranium within the earth. It enters the house through cracks and openings in the foundation. Regularly breathing it can lead to an increased risk of lung cancer. It's important to test for radon – and figure out a mitigation plan if you have a problem – before turning a basement into living space.

Radon detection tests

Radon concentrations can vary widely from house to house on the same block. Always do your own radon test – don't rely on your neighbor's test results. For the most accurate results, use a long-term test. Because it measures levels over several months, it evens out daily fluctuations and provides an accurate gauge of the average radon level in your home. It can also show you if your mitigation efforts are working.

Many people measure radon with a short-term test, which takes about 48 hours. However, these tests provide only a snapshot of time. The results are not as accurate as those from a long-term test.

Reducing radon gas

If your radon test turns up a reading of 4 pCi/l or greater, it's recommended that you hire an EPA certified contractor to reduce the amount of radon entering your house. While sealing cracks and other openings (including sump pits) is an important first step in preventing radon from entering your house, you should also have a system installed to draw the radon from below the house and vent it to the outdoors. Active subslab suction is the most common method. With this, one or more pipes are inserted under the slab and vented to the outside, just like a plumbing vent stack. A fan attached to the pipe helps draw the radon up the pipe. A passive subslab suction system has similar piping but relies on convection, not a fan, to draw the radon to the outdoors. Many new houses have a passive radon venting system built in.

A short-term radon test gives you a snapshot of what the radon levels are in your home on any one day. You can buy one at a home center or from a testing laboratory (make sure it's certified by your state). For a radon detection test to produce accurate results, you must use it precisely as instructed.

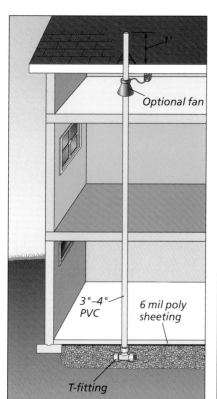
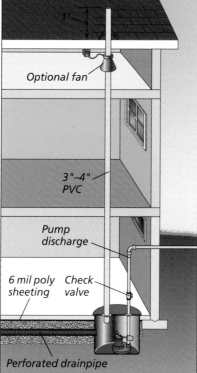

Optional fan

Optional fan

3"–4" PVC

Pump discharge

3"–4" PVC

6 mil poly sheeting

6 mil poly sheeting

Check valve

T-fitting

Perforated drainpipe

A subslab venting system helps prevent radon from entering the house by drawing radon from under the slab and venting it to the outdoors through a PVC pipe. Under the slab the pipe can either terminate with a T-fitting (left) or, if the house has an existing drain tile that empties into a sump pit, the contractor may connect the vent pipe to the sump pit (right) or tie in somewhere along the drain tile. A passive venting system relies on convection to move the gas up the pipe. In an active system, a fan helps vent the radon to the outdoors.

Seal all cracks and holes in the foundation with caulk to help prevent radon from entering the house. If you have a sump pit, it should be covered and made airtight with either a gasket or caulk.

PRELIMINARY ROUGH-INS

Generally, rough-ins don't happen until after the walls are framed. Otherwise, how would you know where the pipes and cables go and what would you attach them to? However, when finishing a basement there are several rough-in tasks that have to be completed before you can begin framing your walls. You need to move anything that will be in the way of the new walls. Typically, that means rerouting any pipes, cables, and ducts that are hung below the joists. If you plan to move or add drain lines below the slab, this is also the time to do that.

Plumbing

Whether your house is old or new, chances are you'll have to move a pipe or two before you can put your walls where you want them.

Moving a drain

A basement bathroom requires drain lines under the concrete floor for a toilet and tub or shower. If your house was built from the 1950s on, there might already be drain lines under the slab. But even so, the builder's plumbing rough-in may not coincide with the layout you want for your bathroom. In this case, the first step is to spend a few hours going over your plans to see if you can come up with a new plan that works just as well, but doesn't involve busting up the slab to move a pipe.

As you make your plans, remember that the drain line must slope ¼ inch for every foot it runs and that pipes can't be embedded in concrete. This means you'll have to place the bathroom pretty near to the existing drain line. You also need to consider venting. Unless you position your bathroom near the existing vent, you'll likely have to run a new vent all the way up through the roof. Be sure to check your local codes to see how far fixtures can be from the stack.

If you can't come up with a new plan, you'll have to move the existing drain lines. Begin the job by laying out the position of the new basement walls on the floor. Then mark the location of the current and future pipe runs on the slab. You need to know exactly which shower or tub and toilet you'll be installing before mapping out the drain lines – the manufacturers provide exact specifications for the clearance between the fixture drain and surrounding walls.

Busting up the slab

First, score along the edges of the opening using a circular saw equipped with a masonry or diamond blade. This helps you keep a clean edge, which will make it easier to do a neat job when it comes to repairing the floor. The saw kicks up a lot of dust and concrete chips; you can keep dust down by having someone

1 *Mark the exact center* of the shower drain opening. Follow the manufacturer's specifications to the letter, paying particular attention to clearances.

2 *Score the concrete* on both sides of the trench before breaking out the concrete. Make a couple of passes with the saw rather than sawing to full depth all at once. Wear a dust respirator plus hearing and eye protection.

3 *Bust out the concrete* with a sledgehammer. Start the hole with a 1-inch steel point, then enlarge the hole with the sledge. As you work, dig out the dirt under the edge of the concrete to make the concrete break more easily. If the project requires a lot of demolition, consider renting an electric jackhammer.

else follow the saw blade's travel with the nozzle of a vacuum. Remove the concrete by smashing it up with a sledgehammer or jackhammer.

Installing the drain

If you're tapping into an existing drain line, you'll need to round up some adapters and transition fittings. This can be confusing since there's an almost overwhelming selection of parts to choose from. In many cases, similar fittings will be able to perform the same job. Talk to somebody knowledgeable about plumbing before you shop.

One of the most commonly used transition fittings is a black neoprene sleeve secured by two adjustable clamp straps. Since these fittings are made to fit drainpipes tightly, a squirt of liquid hand soap on the inside of the fitting will allow you to connect the pieces without too much trouble. Once everything is in position and partially tightened, check your assemblies with a torpedo level for the right pitch. Adjust as necessary, then finish tightening down the clamps that secure the fittings.

If you're installing a drain in a basement without existing plumbing under the slab,

Right tool for the job

Removing or cutting into old pipes often calls for making cuts in tight spaces. A reciprocating saw can usually get you where you need to go. If the space is really tight, try turning the blade upside down. (Remember, always unplug a saw when changing blades.) Here, we reversed the blade and then turned the saw upside down. That way we didn't have to hold the saw at as steep an angle.

Keep in mind that a reciprocating saw has a tendency to kick back when cutting. To keep it under control, always use both hands to hold the saw and set the shoe firmly against the work.

4 *A Y-fitting* *will tie the new shower drain into the existing drain line. Hold a torpedo level against the face of the fitting to check that the pipe has the proper slope (you need a level with a plumb vial to do this). You know you have ¼ inch in 12 when the bubble touches the outside line.*

5 *Make sure that the clearance* *between the drain and the walls is exactly what the fixture manufacturer specifies (use a 2x4 to represent the wall). Here the short pipe is the shower drain and the longer pipe is the beginning of a vent pipe that will hook into the existing vent lines.*

6 *Build a small wood frame* *around the shower drain before patching the floor. The frame will allow you access to the drain.*

7 *Trowel the concrete smooth* *and level with the existing floor after screeding off excess concrete with a piece of 2x4.*

Remove pipes *that will interfere with new framing. If the old pipe is galvanized, cut it out using a reciprocating saw or a hacksaw.*

consult with a professional plumber to design the system. If you hire a plumber to do both the design and the installation work, you can still save money by doing some of the grunt work yourself, such as breaking up the slab and then patching it up once the pipes are installed.

Once the pipes have been laid in the trench, get the work approved by your building inspector. After you get the okay, you can backfill the pipes with sand and then pour in the concrete.

Moving pipes

When existing pipes are in the way of new walls, or are just hanging too low, you'll have to reroute them. Before cutting into existing water pipes, turn off the water and then drain the pipes by opening both the highest and the lowest faucets in the house.

If the existing pipes are galvanized steel, you'll probably find it's easier to cut the pipes apart rather than try to undo them. When galvanized pipes are joined to a threaded fitting, the threads can rust over time and become impossible to undo. In addition, trying to loosen one end of a pipe in a threaded fitting will simply tighten it at the opposite end.

Sewage ejectors

If the building drain runs under the floor, your bathroom fixtures can hook up to that without a problem. But If the main drain exits above the floor, the basement fixtures will be too low to discharge into the sewer line, and you'll need a sewage ejection pump kit. An ejector works by pumping waste up to the sewer line where it can flow out by gravity. You can buy a system that consists of a pump installed in a basin that is recessed into the floor, or one that is enclosed in a tank that sits on top of the slab. One sewage pump will handle the waste from the toilet, sink, and tub/shower – you don't need separate pumps for each fixture. Basement fixtures drain into the basin or tank; as it becomes full, the pump is triggered, and the sewage is pumped up into the regular drain line.

A sewage ejector system *is necessary where bathroom fixtures fall below the sewer line. If there is enough headroom, you can build a subfloor to conceal the tank – just remember to leave access for maintenance.*

Electrical

In a basement project, fixtures and cables that run below the joists will have to be rerouted so you can frame the walls and, eventually, install the ceiling. Rerouting cables will likely mean running at least a few of them through joists. It's okay to drill holes in joists, just remember that it's best to make them along the centerline of the joist – don't make any holes within two inches of the top or bottom of the joist. Make the holes only as large as they need to be to run the cable through, and never larger than one third of the height of the joist. Avoid notching the bottom of the joist. If your house has wood I-beam joists, check the manufacturer's specifications for making holes in the web.

You should have a good understanding of electrical work and code issues before starting any wiring. If you're inexperienced at electrical work, consult a professional. Also, check your local building code to make sure you're allowed to work on your own wiring – in some areas only licensed electricians are allowed to make wiring changes.

1 ***Shut off the power*** *before beginning any work on an electrical system. At the service panel, flip the breaker (or breakers) that turn off power in the area where you'll be working.*

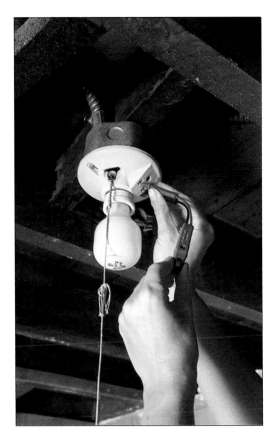

2 ***Test the fixture*** *to make sure the power is off. Insert a probe of a neon tester into each slot of a receptacle. If the bulb on the tester lights up, the power isn't off.*

3 ***Yank out the fixture.*** *If you don't intend to install a new fixture in that location, disconnect the wire from its source – it's against code to conceal a live wire.*

HVAC

The term HVAC is simply an abbreviated way to refer to heat, ventilation, and air conditioning. If there's not already heat in the basement and you live in a cold climate, you'll want to include it in your plans.

Handling existing heating/air-conditioning ductwork in a basement can be challenging. If the ducts reduce headroom, they will probably need to be rerouted (a job for a contractor) or enclosed in a soffit. Talk to the contractor about saving space by substituting round or shallow rectangular ducts for older square ducts. In many remodels, it's possible to design the basement space around the duct-work, and this is the easiest way to go in terms of both time and money. Any remaining exposed ducts can be boxed in with a wood-framed soffit. If the basement ceiling is high enough, you might even be able to conceal the ducts with a suspended ceiling.

Radiant heating

In radiant heating systems, rooms are typically warmed by circuits of tubing embedded in concrete. Hot water circulates through the tubing and radiates heat into the slab; then it is dispersed throughout the room. If you already have hot-water heat and the boiler can handle the extra load, radiant heat might be an option for heating your basement.

Electric radiant-heat systems are an option for areas with milder winters. With these systems, heating wires (sometimes woven into a mat) are embedded in a thin layer of concrete or placed just under the flooring. A separate thermostat controls the heat.

Depending on the type of system you choose, radiant heating can be used to supplement an existing heating system or as a primary source of heat. If you're in the market for a radiant heating system, consult a professional to help you evaluate the cost and efficiency of various systems as well as whether you have the headroom in your basement to accommodate a radiant-heat system.

A new trunk line is needed to supply the new basement rooms, unless your duct system was originally designed to accommodate a finished basement. Moving, adding, or replacing a trunk line is a job for a pro. Forced air heating systems must be carefully balanced or else some rooms will be cold while others are hot.

Six- or 7-inch round ducting is used for branch lines that run between the trunk line and the registers. It may be possible to replace old square ducts with round ducts as long as it doesn't reduce the amount of air that flows through the duct. Check with an HVAC contractor to see if this is a possibility in your home.

FRAMING

Framing a basement *is similar to framing other areas in the home, but there are some interesting twists – most of them related to the foundation and slab. Sometimes you'll have to add or enlarge a window to increase natural light or to provide emergency escape in case of fire. In the course of framing out your basement, you'll typically wind up having to secure wood to concrete, but special fasteners and tools make this job easier than it sounds. You'll also find yourself looking for creative ways to frame out mechanicals that seem to creep into the most inconvenient spaces.*

Egress Windows

If you're going to build a bedroom in your basement, it needs to have an egress window that people can use to escape in case of fire. An egress window is required to have a clear opening of at least 5.7 square feet that is at least 24 inches high and 20 inches wide, and the sill can't be any higher than 44 inches off the floor. If there's not a window of the proper size where you plan to add the bedroom, you'll have to install one.

Installing windows in knee walls

The type of basement you have will affect the work you'll need to do to install an egress window. If yours is a daylight or a walkout basement with a full-height stud wall or knee walls above several courses of masonry block, installing an egress window is like installing a window in any other frame wall.

The first step is to determine whether you need to build a temporary wall to support the house while you make the opening for the new window and frame it out. All of the exterior walls are bearing walls, but there are

1 ***Mark the dimensions*** *of the rough opening on the framing. Follow the manufacturer's specifications for the rough opening of the window you buy. Then mark the center of the opening on the sole plate.*

2 ***Install temporary*** *braces about 4 feet from the wall if you're opening a wall that runs perpendicular to the joists. If the house has floor trusses instead of joists, place the braces under the fasteners that join the web pieces to the lower chord.*

4 ***Pound out the studs*** *with a sledgehammer. You won't be able to pull them out by hand because the sheathing is nailed to them. Wear safety glasses to protect your eyes.*

3 ***Cut the studs*** *from the sole and top plates with a reciprocating saw.*

5 ***Install a king stud*** *on each side of the rough opening, then install the header and the trimmer, or jack, studs that support the header. The header spans the opening and carries the weight of the building above. Any time you remove studs to make an opening in an exterior wall, you must install a header. Header size depends on the load above and the span of the window; consult your building inspector, an engineer, or a licensed contractor.*

bearing walls and then there are bearing walls. Take a look at the joists. If you're making the opening in the wall that runs parallel to the joists, you're probably okay working without a temporary wall. However, if the joists run perpendicular to the wall you're about to tear into, you must build a temporary wall to support the load while you open the wall and frame the window opening.

Installing a window is a two-person job. Windows are heavy and bulky, and a second pair of hands is invaluable when maneuvering the window in the rough opening and later, when shimming and nailing the window in place.

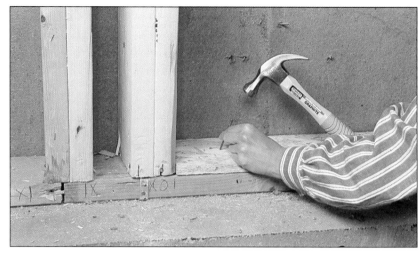

6 *The last piece of framing* for this window is an extra ¾-inch plate along the bottom of the opening. This piece lifts the window slightly, allowing more room for casing along the bottom of the window. If you do this, make sure it won't raise the finished sill height above the 44-inch limit.

7 *Remove enough siding* in the window area to allow room for the nailing flanges that surround fiberglass and clad windows. You can use either a small pry bar or a special zip tool to unlock panels of vinyl siding.

8 *Cut out the sheathing* by running a reciprocating saw around the inside of the rough opening.

9 *Center the window* in the rough opening, loosely nail a corner from the outside, then level the window with shims. Insert the shims from inside the basement so you can get the shims directly under the frame of the window.

10 *Attach a vinyl* or aluminum window to the house by nailing through its flange with 1¾-inch galvanized roofing nails. Read the installation instructions – some windows require caulk around the flanges.

Installing windows in masonry walls

Before breaking a hole through a brick or concrete block foundation wall, consult an engineer to make sure you won't be compromising the strength of the wall.

If the finished sill of the window you're installing will fall below grade, you must install a window well to keep soil and water away from the window. You can make a window well from concrete block or pressure-treated timber, or buy one made of steel or plastic. There are several code requirements for window wells: the horizontal opening has to allow the egress window to open fully, it has to measure at least 36 inches in both directions, and if it's more than 44 inches deep, you have to have a permanent ladder or stairs. Be sure to check your local codes, as well.

Make sure your window well reaches about 8 inches below the windowsill and 4 inches above grade. That will allow room for drainage at the bottom and help prevent water and soil from running in over the top edge.

Don't try to be precise when digging a hole for a window well – you'll need room to move the well around and to fasten it to the foundation walls.

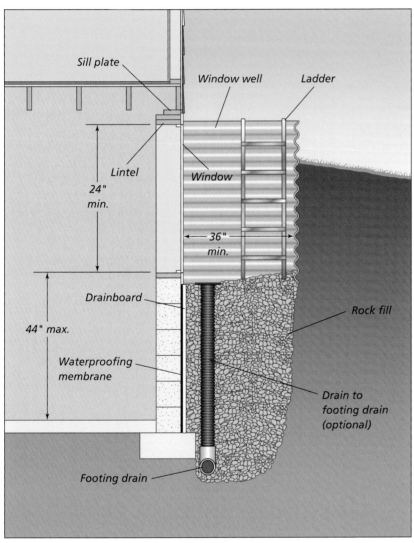

A window well with insufficient drainage is bound to collect water which will leak into your basement. To avoid this, install a drain in the bottom of the window well and connect it to the footing drain. If there is no footing drain, run the drain underground until it can be daylighted somewhere in the yard.

1 **_Cutting a hole in concrete_** _with a power saw is a messy job. You'll be able to see better if someone blows the dust away with a strategically placed fan._

2 **_Finish the rough opening_** _to size by hammering out excess block with a cold chisel and hammer._

Cutting through

Cut a hole in a brick or block wall using a circular saw fitted with a masonry blade. Make the opening several inches taller and wider than the rough opening specified for your new window. (Pressure-treated 2x10 or 2x12 bucks are attached to the masonry before the window is installed.) Score both sides, then cut through, working slowly so you don't overheat the saw. A rented gas-powered concrete saw with a diamond blade works well, too. Be sure to wear a dust respirator, hearing protectors, and safety glasses when cutting concrete.

3 *Attach the window casing* to the bucks with galvanized deck screws. Use pressure-treated lumber for the bucks and the casing.

4 *If using aluminum-clad* windows, fit the aluminum pieces to the wood window casing. You may be able to have a contractor do the cladding only.

5 *Position the window well* and mark the mounting holes on the foundation wall. The top of the well should be at least 4 inches above grade.

6 *Anchor the window well* to the foundation wall with masonry fasteners. Shovel some gravel into the bottom of the well for drainage, and backfill around the window well with gravel topped with soil.

7 *Install a ladder* if the well depth exceeds 44 inches. Code requires that the ladder be permanently attached. If there is space, built-in steps are an option, as well.

Furring Out Masonry Walls

Most houses have poured concrete or concrete block for at least some of the basement walls, so in a basement remodel you'll have to fur out the masonry walls so you can attach the drywall and to allow room for insulation, outlets, and switches.

Moisture barriers

Before you start framing, check whether your local regulations call for a moisture barrier. A moisture barrier is polyethylene sheeting that goes between the masonry and the framing. In most parts of the country, moisture barriers are recommended to keep moisture that seeps through the foundation from penetrating the insulation and rotting the framing or drywall. Some building codes call for a vapor barrier (which goes over the insulation and under the drywall) instead of a moisture barrier. This is to prevent vapor in the air from passing through the drywall into the insulation and framing. Some areas will require both a moisture barrier and a vapor barrier. (The wisdom of this requirement is being debated as any moisture that does make it through either the moisture barrier or the vapor barrier will be trapped where it can do the most harm.)

Furring materials

You can use 2x2s, 2x3s, or 2x4s to fur out masonry walls. Furring with 2x4s provides more room for insulation and makes it a lot easier to do the electrical work. With 2x2 furring, you can't fit in quite as much insulation and you have to use shallow boxes for

1 *Assembling walls on a level surface,* such as a basement slab, and raising them into place helps speed along the framing. A partition wall will abut the 2x6 laid flat at the end of this wall. The wall will be fastened to the masonry with concrete nails driven through the 2x4 nailers, not through the 2x2 top plate.

2 *Tilt the wall up* into position. Half-height walls are easy. If you're tilting up a full-height wall, remove any obstacles (like light bulbs) that may be in the upward path.

3 *Secure the sole plate* using either a powder-actuated nailer or concrete nails and a hammer. The sole plate should be pressure-treated lumber.

the electrical work. However, 2x2 furring chews up less floor space.

If you have knee walls over top of half-height masonry walls, you have a few more choices to make. You can raise 2x4 walls from floor to ceiling, eliminating the ledge where the masonry meets the knee wall, you can fur out the masonry with 2x2s and finish the resulting ledge with drywall or wood, or you can fur out the masonry with 2x4s to create a ledge that is deep enough to support shelving above.

Building the walls

Whichever material you choose, you can either build each wall on the slab and raise it into place as a unit, or stick-frame the wall in place. Building the walls on your basement floor lets you work faster, but you will need an extra pair of hands when it comes time to tip a floor-to-ceiling wall up into place. Build the wall ¼ inch shorter than the actual clearance, or it will catch on the joists when you try to raise it up. The wall gets shimmed to secure it in place. Construction adhesive and powder-driven nails secure the sole plate. Use concrete nails to fasten the wood framing to the concrete walls; run the nails into the mortar joints if the foundation is made from block.

When stick-framing, first secure the sole plate with construction adhesive and a powder-actuated nailer, then use a plumb bob to locate the top plate. Snap a line along the joists, then nail up the top plate. Toenail the ends of each stud to the plates.

Whether you're building walls on the floor or in place, make sure that all your framing is straight, secure, and spaced 16 inches on center. For a good drywall job later, the nailing faces of the studs should all be flush and aligned in a level plane. Don't use excessively bowed or crooked studs.

How it works

A powder-actuated nailer anchors wood framing to masonry by firing nails like a gun fires bullets. There's some debate over whether using this tool can cause cracks in the slab, but no definite answers. If you'll be using a powder-actuated nailer, make sure to wear hearing protection – this tool is loud. Always wear safety glasses when driving nails, whether with a hammer or a nailer.

4 *Plumb each wall* before securing it. Note the kickers that attach the furring to the kneewall. These will also provide a nailing surface for the ledge material to be installed later.

5 *Use concrete nails* – not a powder-actuated nailer – when fastening furring to block walls. Drive the nails into the mortar joints as low as possible; avoid driving nails in the top couple of inches of the joint.

1 ***Frame the walls*** *about ¼ inch short to keep them from getting hung up on the joists when you tip them up.*

2 ***Make sure*** *the wall is plumb before attaching it to the ceiling joists and slab. Check several different studs along the wall.*

Partition Walls

Partition walls divide the basement space into useful areas. If you're bringing in big items, such as oversize whirlpool tubs, appliances, or HVAC equipment, it's helpful to get these in place before putting up the partition walls.

Like exterior walls, partition walls can be built in place or framed on the floor and tipped up into position. Although you save time with floor-built walls, there may be some situations where pipes or beams will interfere with tilting up a wall. In these cases, you may find it easiest to stick-frame the walls in place.

Stick-framing is also a good option if you have an older house that has settled unevenly. Attach the sole and top plates, then measure for and install the studs one at a time. This will accommodate the variations in height from one end of the wall to the other.

Whichever way you frame the walls, locate partition walls along two chalklines, one on the floor and one on the joists. Use a plumb bob to locate the top plate once the position of the sole plate has been snapped. When nailing the sole plate along the line on a slab, first put down a bead of construction adhesive, then use a powder-actuated nailer to drive nails every 16 inches.

Walls that run perpendicular to the ceiling joists or trusses can be nailed to the framing above with 16d nails. When a wall runs parallel to the joists, you'll need to install 2x4 blocking between joists and nail the top plate to the blocking unless, through sheer luck or

New life for old joists

Joists that are cracked, twisted, sagging, or otherwise damaged should be strengthened by a process called sistering before framing the partition walls. Since the floor sheathing above is nailed to the tops of the joists, it's never a good idea to remove a joist, even if it appears to be badly damaged.

Sistering is simply a matter of cutting a new joist to the same size as the damaged joist and attaching it to the old joist with construction adhesive and 16d nails or carriage bolts. Place the fasteners in a W pattern. Try to keep the fasteners within ¾ inch of the joist edges. Make sure the new joist is supported in the same way as the damaged joist.

good planning, the wall is directly under a joist. You'll also need to install blocking between studs if another wall will abut it.

If your wall is going to have a doorway, you'll need to frame a rough opening to the specifications of the door manufacturer. In partition walls, the header is supported on each side by a jack stud – if there's room, cripple studs span the space between the header and the top plate. If you're framing on the floor, run the sole plate the full width of the wall and cut out the extra later. This will make the wall more rigid and easier to handle when you tip it up.

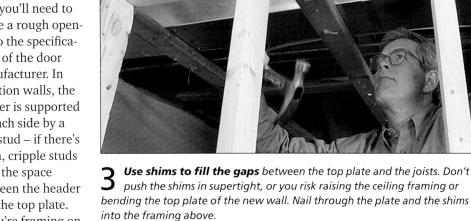

3 *Use shims to fill the gaps* between the top plate and the joists. Don't push the shims in supertight, or you risk raising the ceiling framing or bending the top plate of the new wall. Nail through the plate and the shims into the framing above.

Install nailers or blocking wherever two partition walls will butt together. Note how the sole plate has been notched to fit around the drainpipe.

Where two walls meet, nail them together. Note the special construction of this partition wall. The last full-height stud is fastened to a 2x6 in the furring, while the half-stud rests on the block and is nailed to a stud in the knee wall.

Nail 2x4 blocking between studs wherever a partition wall will butt. The blocking also provides a nailing surface for drywall.

Make sure the wall is plumb by checking several different studs along the wall. Where there is a doorway, saw out the sole plate in the threshold area. When doing tip-up framing, it's easiest to frame up the wall with a full sole plate and then cut out the excess.

Framing with steel studs

Light gauge steel studs are being used more and more often for framing partition walls. The studs and tracks are light, straight, and unlikely to rust since the steel is galvanized. You can use 33-, 27-, or 18-mil steel studs and tracks for non-bearing walls.

To frame a wall, screw the top track to the joists and anchor the bottom track to the slab with construction adhesive and powder-actuated nails. Use #8 self-drilling low-profile screws to fasten the studs to the tracks (you only need one screw at the top and bottom of each stud). To cut the studs to length use a circular saw with a carbide-tipped blade, aviation snips, or a special tool called a nibbler.

The studs have prepunched holes every 24 inches for pipes and cables. You have to install grommets in the holes to protect the cable sheathing and, if you run copper pipe, you'll have to put a barrier between the pipe and the stud to prevent the corrosion that happens when different metals are in contact. Short lengths of foam pipe insulation work well for this.

To hang drywall, use #6 or #8 sharp-point screws instead of drywall screws. (You can also use these screws to hang pictures.) Attach trim moldings to the drywall with glue. (You can tack the molding in place with pneumatic staples until the glue dries.)

Install blocking to support jamb extensions. With deep-set windows you will probably have to install jamb extensions to trim out the window. Order these when you order the window.

ROUGH-INS

Making a basement space livable means that your home's mechanical systems – HVAC, plumbing, and wiring – all must be evaluated and the decision made whether to do the work yourself or hire some or all of it out. In some areas, your local building code will make your decisions for you, requiring licensed professionals to do some types of work.

Some framing tasks must wait until after the rough-ins are done. One big issue in basements, for example, is how to conceal beams, posts, pipes, and ductwork. Another is transforming a standard-issue basement stairway into something both safe and visually appealing.

HVAC

If you're tapping into a hot-air system to heat a small basement space, you may be able to splice a new duct into the existing ductwork without too much trouble. Just be careful not to tie into the main system too close to the heat source because if the hot air is diverted early on, there may not be enough to heat the rest of the house effectively. If you'll be heating a large space, or several rooms on the lower level – and the system wasn't designed for future basement finishing – or if you'll need to reroute ductwork, talk to an HVAC professional before proceeding. Dealing with large ducts can be complex and requires special tools and skills. Balancing a heating system can be difficult even for pros.

Hot-water baseboard heat can usually be easily extended to service basement living areas, provided the boiler has the capacity. You might want to add another zone to the system to accommodate the basement area.

This way you will be able to turn down the thermostat – and save energy – when the space is not occupied.

Installing an independent electric baseboard heating system is a reasonable option if you can't – or don't want to – tie into your existing system. Just make sure the system won't overload the service panel. Recessed electric convector units are also useful in basements.

Fabricating large ducts to service a basement living area is best left to a professional.

Tying a new baseboard radiator into an existing hot-water heating system is usually no problem. The contractor will make sure that the boiler has enough capacity and that the new baseboard radiator is appropriately sized to heat the room.

Flexible ducting can be easily run through trusses, but if your ceiling is framed with joists, you will likely have to conceal it inside a soffit.

Plumbing Overview

Aplumbing system is made up of two components: a water supply system that brings fresh water into the house and a drainage system that carries wastewater away.

The supply system

The house supply system starts at the water meter and shutoff valve. The water remains in a single pipe until it reaches the water heater, then it splits into two lines. One carries cold water and another passes through the water heater and carries hot water. The pipes run parallel throughout the house carrying water to each fixture. The water is pressurized to make sure that the flow is sufficient.

Because supply pipes are fairly small in diameter and the water is under pressure, you can run supply lines just about anywhere. They can run vertically and horizontally, and can turn 90-degree corners.

The DWV system

The drainage system is composed of two sets of pipes: drains and vents. A vertical soil stack (your house may have more than one) rises from the sewer line in the basement straight out through the roof. Fixtures like sinks and toilets drain through waste pipes and into the soil stack. Drainage pipes aren't under pressure, so horizontal pipes must slope in order to drain properly.

Each fixture (everything that has a drain) has to have a vent line. The vent pipes in a drainage system release gases into the main stack, where they rise up and out to dissipate outdoors. The vent system keeps the air pressure within the system constant so wastewater can drain freely.

Every fixture also has a trap in its drain line. The trap holds a small amount of water which prevents sewer gases from seeping into the house. The vent system keeps the traps from being sucked dry when the fixtures drain.

When you do the plumbing rough-in, start with the drain and vent pipes, then tackle the supply lines. It's easier to maneuver small pipes around large pipes than vice versa.

In a snap

If your rough-in plans call for cutting into an existing cast-iron soil stack or drain line, your best bet is to pick up a cast-iron cutter at the rental center. To use it, wrap the chain of cutter wheels around the pipe, connect it to the handle, hand tighten the chain, then crank only until the pipe snaps. Before you cut a cast-iron soil stack, make sure it is supported with clamps. Be sure to wear gloves and safety glasses when cutting cast-iron pipe. It's very brittle and if it shatters, the shards are very sharp.

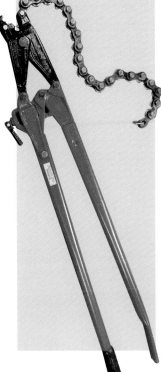

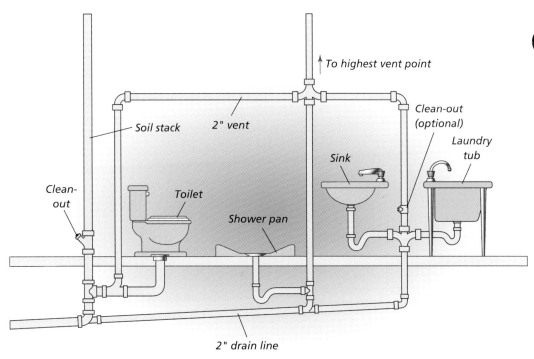

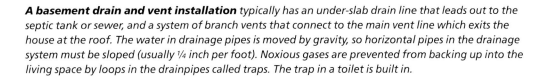

A basement drain and vent installation typically has an under-slab drain line that leads out to the septic tank or sewer, and a system of branch vents that connect to the main vent line which exits the house at the roof. The water in drainage pipes is moved by gravity, so horizontal pipes in the drainage system must be sloped (usually ¼ inch per foot). Noxious gases are prevented from backing up into the living space by loops in the drainpipes called traps. The trap in a toilet is built in.

About solvent glues

Don't grab just any solvent cement to glue plastic pipe. Always use products made specifically for the plastic you are gluing, or else use a universal solvent cement. Never use a primer with ABS, although you can apply cleaner before applying the solvent cement. With PCV and CPVC, you do prime the joint first. The primer cleans the pipe and softens the plastic for a faster stronger weld – the purple color confirms to the inspector that you've used primer. Then you apply the solvent cement, which welds the pieces together.

Gluing Plastic Pipe

Plastic pipe is the standard in drain systems and some local codes also allow it to be used in supply lines. Be sure to check your local code to see what's allowed. The plastic may be PVC, CPVC, or ABS – all abbreviations for chemical composition. PVC is used for drain lines, vents, and cold-water supply lines; CPVC is used for both hot and cold supply lines; ABS is used only for drain lines and vents. You can connect plastic pipe to galvanized pipe, but you need to buy a special transition fitting. Likewise, you can connect different types of plastic pipe together using special fittings.

Always test-fit pieces of plastic pipe before gluing them together, but don't force the pipe ends into the fittings or you may not be able to pull them out again. When it's time to glue the joint, the cement will act as a lubricant, allowing the pipe to seat properly in the fitting.

1 **Drill through the framing** to accommodate new pipes, making the holes slightly larger than the pipes. In a load-bearing 2x4, the maximum hole size is 1⁷⁄₁₆ inches (a diameter of 2 inches is okay in a non-load-bearing stud).

2 **Measure carefully** for the length of pipe, remembering to account for the portions of the pipe that will fit inside the fittings. Inside the fitting is a shoulder, which the pipe should seat against. Cut the pipe with a hacksaw or a power miter saw. The cut should be square to fit flush against the shoulder.

3 **Scrape all the burrs** from the cut end of the pipe with a utility knife or a file. Burrs can weaken the bond between the solvent cement and the pipe.

4 **Coat the inside of the fitting** and the outside of the pipe end with solvent cement. PVC and CPVC pipes need to be primed, but ABS pipe should only be glued with the self-priming solvent cement formulated for it.

5 **Join the pieces** and rotate them about ¼ turn as you push them together to spread the glue around. Hold the pieces together for about 30 seconds until the glue grabs. When the slope and/or the angle of the fitting is critical, align the pieces and make a mark across both pieces when test-fitting. When it's time to make the connection, insert the pipe so the marks are a quarter turn off, then turn to align the marks.

Soldering Copper

Soldering, or sweating, copper joints isn't a difficult job, but it does require care and cleanliness. It's important to start out with clean pipes because flux and solder won't stick well to oily or dirty surfaces. Even the oil left by a fingertip can be enough to prevent a good bond.

Solder that won't melt may be an indication that the inside of the pipe is wet. Pipes that aren't absolutely dry won't heat up enough to melt the solder.

After you're finished soldering the joint and it's cooled a bit, wipe it off with a damp rag. This removes excess flux that would eventually corrode the copper and it makes a neat looking joint.

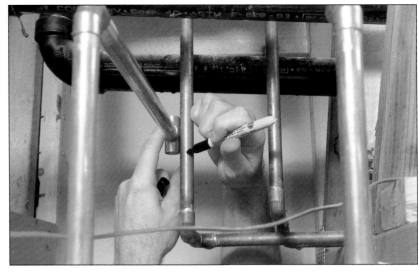

1 *Measure the area to be cut by holding up a T-fitting to the pipe. There are mathematical ways to figure length, but using the actual fittings and pipe is easiest.*

2 *Cut copper pipe to length with a tubing cutter. Turn the cutter around the pipe, tightening the knob after each turn until it cuts through the pipe.*

3 *Polish the pipe end with emery cloth, not steel wool. Steel wool will leave fibers on the pipe.*

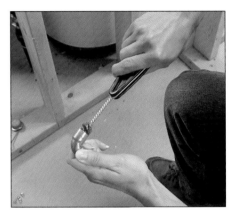

4 *Run a steel brush around the inside of the fitting to remove all grease, dirt, and oxidation.*

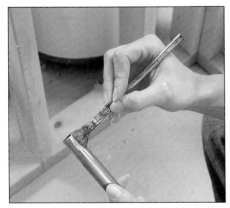

5 *Brush a coat of flux on the outside of the pipe end and the inside of the fitting. To spread the flux evenly, join the pieces and gently twist them back and forth several times.*

6 *Hold the torch to the joint, moving it back and forth so you don't burn off the flux. Touch the solder to the joint. When you see the solder start to melt, pull the flame away from the pipe. The solder will spread around the joint by capillary action.*

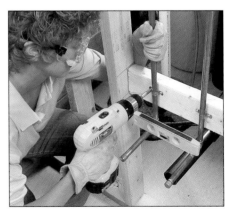

7 *Pipe stub-outs must be firmly anchored with tube straps. You should also support horizontal and vertical pipe runs. Check your local codes for spacing of the supports.*

Wiring Basics

In a basement remodel you'll probably be able to extend the existing circuits to accommodate new lighting, but sometimes (such as when adding a major appliance), you'll have to add new circuits. Check your local building code to see if you need the services of a licensed electrician for this. Remember, doing electrical work without a required permit is illegal and may also invalidate your homeowner's insurance.

Codes specify where you must put switches and receptacles. Switches usually go 48 to 50 inches above the floor; receptacles are typically positioned 12 to 18 inches above the floor.

Your local code will also specify the materials that are allowed. Wiring in most areas will be done with either 14/2 or 12/2 Type NM (nonmetallic-sheathed) cable. The first number refers to the gauge, or diameter, of the wire (the lower the number, the larger the wire). The second number tells how many conducting wires are in the cable. However, in some areas armored cable or metal conduit is required. The code will also specify whether plastic or metal boxes should be used.

Wiring boxes in shallow walls

If you're using 2x2 furring strips instead of 2x4 studs to frame out foundation walls, you won't have the depth you need to use standard-sized electrical boxes. Instead, buy shallow, or pancake, boxes. These are only 1½ inches deep, but they are wider to accommodate the cables. Be careful when using these boxes, because the size and number of cables that can be contained within them are regulated by box size in cubic inches.

1 *Nail electrical boxes* to the studs indicated on your electrical plan. A mark on the side of each box shows how far it should stick out past the framing so that its front will end up flush with the drywall.

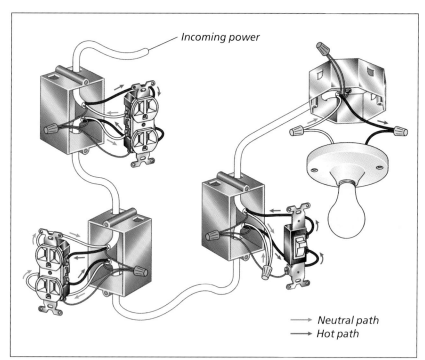

Incoming power

→ Neutral path
➔ Hot path

Electricity needs a completed circuit to work properly – a way out through the hot wire and a way back through the neutral wire. In an electrical circuit, the hot wires, which usually have black or red insulation, deliver power to a device. The electricity completes the circuit on the neutral wires, which are most often white. In this circuit, the wires coming from the service panel are hooked to an outlet, which relays power to the next outlet, which relays power to the switch and light.

2 *Run cable to the boxes* from the panel or from an existing circuit. Feed the cable through holes drilled through the framing.

Memory aid

When you have several cables coming into a box, don't trust that you will remember which cable goes where when it comes time to hook up the fixtures. After all, that could be weeks from now. It's best to label the cable ends now with a permanent marker. If you've already stripped off the sheathing, slip a scrap over the wire ends and label that.

3 **Use a cable stripper** to remove sheathing from a cable. Place the stripper over the cable and squeeze the handles as you pull the tool down the end of the cable. Then peel off the sheathing and cut it with a utility knife.

4 **Feed the cable** into the electrical box. Sheathing must extend at least ¼ inch – but not more than 1 inch – into the box. Both plastic and metal boxes come with thin sections called knockouts. You'll have to knock these out with a screwdriver so you can feed the cable into the box.

5 **Fasten the cable to the framing** every 4½ feet. Add a staple where the cable turns and just before cable enters an electrical box; the staple must be within 12 inches of the box.

6 **Coil the cable** to fit into the electrical box. Leave a minimum of 6 inches of extra cable at each box for making connections. A length of 8 inches makes it easier to make connections, but may be more difficult to stuff into the box.

Nail the brackets on the recessed light to the ceiling joists. If you're sound-proofing the ceiling with insulation, be sure to buy fixtures rated for insulation contact.

Connect the light fixture according to the manufacturer's schematic. Since all the lights in this installation are controlled by one switch, power is brought in, fed to the light, then carried along to the next light.

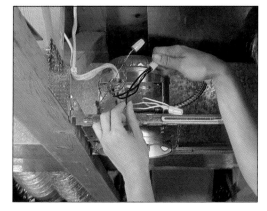

An insulated duct carries moist bathroom air outdoors. Ducts can be flexible or rigid and many systems use a combination of both – flexible to get around obstacles, and rigid for the straight runs.

Wiring Projects

Most wiring projects are done in two stages: rough-in and trim-out. During the rough-in you install the electrical boxes and run the wire into them. Trim-out is when you install the fixtures, switches, and receptacles at the end of the job. The exception is recessed lighting. With recessed lights you make the connections at the rough-in stage, because the fixture itself is buried in the ceiling.

In many homes, just a small amount of light enters a lower level. For this reason, a well-designed lighting scheme is necessary. A good lighting plan will help you turn a dark cave into a bright, livable space. Keep headroom in mind when working on your lighting design. If headroom is an issue, recessed lights and wall sconces are good choices.

If your basement remodel includes a bathroom, and the bathroom doesn't have a window, you will be required by code to install a power ventilator. Even if your bathroom does have a window, you should install a vent fan – it's faster and more efficient at removing moisture. Your electrical code will also require GFCI (ground-fault circuit interrupter) outlets in the bathroom and other wet areas.

As computer and home entertainment technology continues to advance, home offices and home media centers are becoming more popular. Even if you don't have high-tech equipment at the moment, you can save

The fan blower and housing mount in the ceiling. The fan and grille get mounted when the project is almost done. Fans are sized by the amount of air they can move measured in cubic feet per minute (CFM). Codes typically require at least eight air changes per hour.

yourself a lot of trouble later by planning for the equipment you eventually might acquire. It makes sense to prewire for TVs, computers, and home theater speakers during the rough-in phase of a project.

Home offices typically require outlets for computers, fax machines, copiers, and printers. In addition, don't skimp on your phone wiring. At least two separate phone lines are typically required – one for family calls and one to handle business calls. The expense of a third line to handle the computer modem can often be justified by the intended use.

Your home should already have a smoke detector on every floor – install one on the basement level, too. If there's a bedroom, locate another smoke detector inside the bedroom door, as required by code. A carbon monoxide detector is also a necessity, especially if people will be sleeping in the basement.

Consider running a conduit of PVC pipe from the service panel to any room where you (or later occupants) may want to run cable in the future. Keep 90-degree elbows to a minimum – and use wide sweep fittings where you do need 90-degree turns – otherwise it may be difficult to pull cable through the conduit.

240-volt circuits may be required for some appliances, such as dryers, water heaters, and electric baseboard heaters. The cable has two hot leads, one black and one red, and is usually a heavier gauge, but you run it the same way as any other wire. However, you may need an electrician to make the connection at the panel.

Smoke detectors for new construction or a remodel must be hardwired. When one trips, all the smoke detectors go off so there's no chance of sleeping through an alarm that goes off in another part of the house.

Install communications wiring now, even if you won't use it right away. The blue Category 5, or CAT 5, cable contains four sets of twisted-pair phone wires. Twisted-pair wiring reduces electronic interference in the lines. Here, it will connect a household computer network. The gray cable can serve two phone lines.

Use your pull

A piece of string threaded through a PVC conduit – and left there – will make it easier to wire additional equipment at a later date. You just tie the cable to the string and pull it through the conduit from the other end.

To get the string in place, make a small balloon out of a piece of sandwich bag, tie it off with the end of the string, and stuff the balloon into the conduit end. Have somebody at the other end of the conduit start up a vacuum. As the balloon is sucked through the conduit, feed the string through behind it. After the balloon has exited the other end, cut the string a little long and leave it in the conduit for future use. Feed in another piece of string whenever you pull cable so you will always have a string in there for pulling new cable.

Nail fireblocking between studs at the same height as the bottom of the soffit. It should be the same dimension as the studs.

Fiberglass insulation is also an acceptable fireblocking material. It's fast and easy to install, especially when filling openings around pipes, ducts, and wires.

Soffits

Beams are an essential part of the structure of any basement. They support the floor joists and can't be removed without damaging the structural integrity of the house. If they intrude into your planned living space, you may be able to conceal them within a suspended ceiling. If there's not enough headroom for this, you'll have to conceal them with a soffit. Soffits are also used to conceal pipes and ductwork. Before nailing any lumber in place, check that it is straight. Assemble the soffit on the floor, then lift it into position and fasten it to marks made on the joists.

Fire blocks

Fire blocks (also called fire stops) help prevent a fire in a wall or ceiling from spreading to other areas of the house through the joist and stud cavities. Concealed areas created by soffits and dropped ceilings must have fireblocking. This can be done by blocking between wall studs at the bottom level of the soffit with wood. Use 2x blocking that is the same dimensions as the studs. Since lumber varies in dimension, make sure your blocking is flush with the wall studs. Wider blocking will cause trouble when you're installing drywall or other finish material.

You can also use mineral or fiberglass insulation batts – not loosefill insulation – as fireblocking. When used as a fireblocking, insulation should be packed tightly into the opening.

Another option is to install drywall, ½-inch plywood, or oriented strand board (OSB) sheathing on either the wall or ceiling side of the soffit. In addition, fireblocking should be installed at 10-foot intervals in both horizontal and vertical soffits.

Construction options

There are several ways to build a soffit, but you must make sure that the soffit will not interfere with the headroom in the living space. Check your building code – most require that there be at least 84 inches of headroom underneath a beam. If ductwork for heating or air conditioning runs along a beam, the job will look neater if you use one soffit to frame both obstructions.

In addition to the options shown here, beams can be boxed out with ½-inch plywood attached to wooden cleats. Paneling or solid wood can also be substituted for the plywood.

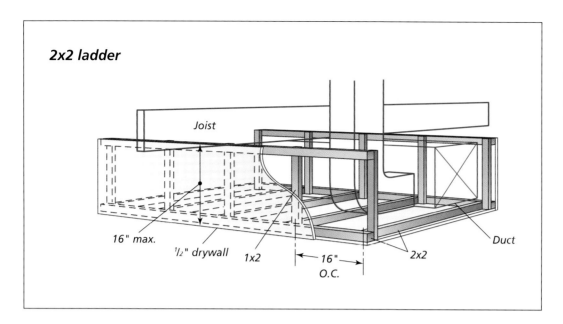

2x2 ladder

Joist

16" max.

$1/2$" drywall

1x2

16"
O.C.

2x2

Duct

Ladders of 2x2s make up the traditional soffit. The ladder soffit utilizes inexpensive materials but it can take more time to build. The 2x2s tend to warp or twist more than other materials.

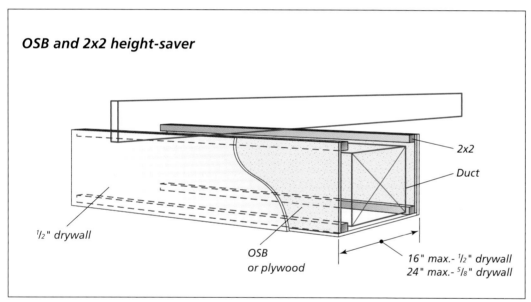

OSB and 2x2 height-saver

2x2

Duct

$1/2$" drywall

OSB or plywood

16" max.- $1/2$" drywall
24" max.- $5/8$" drywall

Heightsaver soffits let you keep the bottoms of the soffits as high as possible to save headroom. Panels made from a 2x2 frame and OSB are attached to the joists. There's no framing across the bottom – only drywall. You can span up to 2 feet if you use $5/8$-inch drywall.

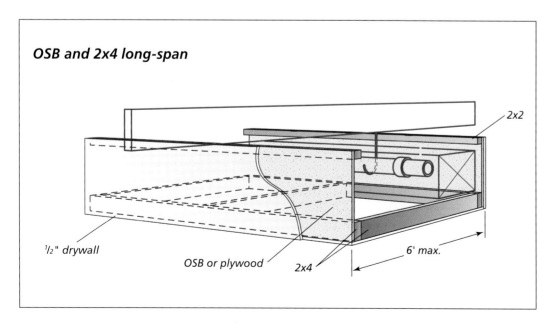

OSB and 2x4 long-span

2x2

$1/2$" drywall

OSB or plywood

2x4

6' max.

Long-span soffits are made from 2x4s and OSB. Using 2x4s instead of 2x2s gives the soffits the strength they need to span up to 6 feet. The sides are OSB covered with drywall, while the bottom is covered with a layer of drywall.

Subfloor Framing

Concrete floors can be painted or, if the slab is smooth and dry, tile, vinyl, carpet, plastic-laminate, or engineered wood flooring can be installed directly over the concrete. However, some people find the floor too hard and cold when flooring is installed right over the slab. The solution most often considered is a subfloor. A subfloor will provide cushioning – and add warmth if you insulate it – to the basement floor. Your building department may have something to say about basement flooring. Some codes, for example, may require that fire blocks must be placed between wood sleepers.

Build the subfloor from pressure-treated 2x4s laid flat to save headroom. Lay the perimeter sleepers first, then fill in between them with the 2x4s positioned every 16 inches on center. If the floor is uneven, use shims to level the sleepers. Lay the insulation between the sleepers, then cover everything with a polyethylene vapor barrier. (Some codes require a moisture barrier under the sleepers instead of a vapor barrier over them, so be sure to check your local codes.) When installing the plywood subfloor, run the panels perpendicular to the sleepers, staggering the joints. Fasten the plywood with nails or screws every 6 inches along the panel edges and every 12 inches in the field.

1 *Fasten the sleepers* to the slab with construction adhesive and a powder-actuated nailer or with concrete nails long enough to penetrate about an inch into the slab. Longer nails are harder to drive and won't substantially increase holding power.

2 *Install batts of unfaced fiberglass* insulation between the sleepers. You can use rigid insulation, but it doesn't conform to the sleepers the way batts do so there will be small air gaps between the panels and the sleepers.

3 *Spread a polyethylene vapor barrier* over the sleepers and insulation. Overlap the seams and seal them with tape.

4 *Lay the plywood perpendicular* to the sleepers. Fasten the plywood to the sleepers with 6d ring shank nails, 8d common nails, or 2-inch screws.

Staircase Anatomy

The stairs in your basement may not be where you want them or they may not conform to your building code. Codes typically are quite specific about stair construction and your project will not pass inspection if the stairs don't measure up.

Most codes will require that risers not exceed 8 inches in height (7 inches is ideal), and they can't vary more than ⅜ inch per step. Treads must be no shallower than 9 inches. Typically, nosings shouldn't protrude over risers more than 1½ inches. The width of the stair must be at least 36 inches.

Headroom is another consideration. Again, check your building code, but typically there must be at least 80 inches of headroom between the stair nosing and the ceiling above.

Any stairway with four or more steps must have a handrail positioned 34 to 38 inches above the stair nosing. Code also requires that the handrail's shape is graspable and between 1¼ and 2 inches wide.

If your stair will have a landing, it has to be at least 3 feet by 3 feet and should be the same width as the stairs.

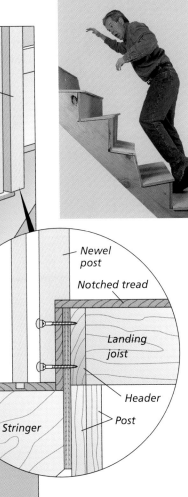

Header, Landing joist, Riser, ³/₄" plywood, Tread, Post, Stringer

Landing newel post

Handrail

Tread

Riser

Pressure-treated stringer plate

Middle Stringer

Newel post

Balusters

Newel post, Notched tread, Landing joist, Header, Post, Stringer

There are several ways to frame a staircase, but the basic components are the same. We assemble a carriage composed of three stringers connected to a plywood stringer header and a pressure-treated stringer plate, and then attach the stringer header to the landing header. (The landing is supported by the wall framing and a 4x4 post.) After attaching the risers and treads, we attach the newel posts. Note that both the landing newel post and the landing nosing are notched. The balusters have pegged bottoms to fit in holes in the treads, while the tops fit into holes in the underside of the handrail. The balusters can be spaced no more than 4 inches apart.

Additional Framing Tasks

Circular stairs

A circular or spiral stair can add visual interest to the practical function of going between lower and upper levels. There are several styles available. The ones with tight curves and steep stairs take up less floor space, but are usually much less inviting to use than those with wider stairs and gentler climbs. They also make it difficult – or impossible – to move large items into or out of the basement.

What's the difference between a spiral and a circular stair? A spiral staircase coils around a straight or curved central pole while a circular stair typically ascends in one wide curve. You can buy spiral stairs prefabricated or in kit form in metal or wood. Circular stairs must generally be custom-built for the space, and are usually made out of wood. Since building codes vary depending on the area, check with an official from your building department before proceeding with a curved stair. Once you've got the approval, check with the retailer to determine the best size and model stairway for your project.

Before you put down your hammer, finish off the odd jobs before moving on to insulating and finishing the walls. If you'll be drywalling your basement walls and ceiling, check that you have something to nail the drywall to at every corner. Add nailers wherever necessary. In addition, check that wires and pipes that fall toward the edge of a stud or joist are properly protected with metal plates. Nonmetallic-sheathed cable within 1¼ inches of a stud must have a nail plate, but why take chances? Put plates anywhere you're likely to drive a nail or screw through a pipe or a cable.

Also at this point, think about adding little extras to your framing project. The area underneath a staircase, for example, can be easily transformed from wasted space into a roomy closet or storage area. It's a simple matter to add shelves or install roll-out bins. If the stairs are straight, there might be access from both sides, while stairs built in an L-configuration can offer space for individual niches or cubbyholes.

Install blocking *for pedestal sinks and grab bars while the wall is still open. Grab bars and sinks have to be supported by solid blocking – they can't simply be screwed into studs or furring strips or they might pull out.*

Short pieces of 2x2 *installed between joists or studs make good nailers. Check all the ceiling and wall edges to make sure there's something there to fasten the drywall to.*

Nail a metal protector plate *on the stud anywhere that a wire or a pipe is within 1¼ inches of the edge of a stud. Most codes specify that the plate be a minimum of ⅟₁₆ inch thick.*

INSULATION and DRYWALL

Once the building inspector *has signed off on your framing and mechanical rough-ins, you can move on to the insulation and drywall. Insulating the walls of a basement and finishing them off with drywall use techniques that apply to remodeling elsewhere in the house, but there are still some basement-related twists to each of these jobs. Insulation and drywall often require inspections; check with your building department to see what's required in your area.*

Insulation

How you insulate your basement pretty much depends on what's already been done to the house and the local building codes that apply. Pay particular attention to specifications on vapor barriers, which differ from area to area.

If the basement walls have been furred out with 2x2s, use rigid insulation to insulate the walls. It takes some fitting and trimming to get the insulation boards to fit snug, but the effort pays off in increased energy efficiency. Because 2x2s are rarely straight, you'll probably end up with gaps between the 2x2s and the insulation. You can fill these with nonexpanding foam insulation. Make sure the foam is compatible with the insulation you are using.

If the foundation walls have been framed with 2x3s or 2x4s, you can insulate with batts of fiberglass insulation. Use unfaced batts and tuck them gently between the studs. Don't compress the insulation – the insulating value comes from the pockets of air trapped between fibers. Squeezing out the air pockets reduces the effectiveness of the insulation.

Use scraps of fiberglass insulation or expanding spray foam to fill any gaps, particularly those around pipes or wires that exit the exterior walls. Avoid using expanding foam around windows and doors, because the foam can bow out the wood jambs. Be careful when spraying the foam – it sometimes expands faster and to a greater volume than you expect.

Install a vapor barrier of 4- or 6-mil polyethylene over the insulation. Fasten the vapor barrier to the studs with a hammer stapler, but don't overstaple – too many holes compromise the effectiveness of the vapor barrier. You don't need to tape seams, but they should be overlapped.

Place batts of fiberglass insulation *in the cavities between studs. Use unfaced batts – you'll be covering the insulation with a vapor barrier later.*

Cut pieces of 1½-inch-thick rigid foam insulation *to fit between the 2x2 furring fastened to the masonry walls. Fill gaps around electrical boxes located on exterior walls with expanding foam.*

To reduce sound transmission *through the ceiling, place fiberglass insulation in the joist cavities. This will cut noise to – and from – the rooms above the basement. Insulation supports hold the batts between joists.*

Soundproofing

Depending upon how the finished basement will be used, you may want to add some soundproofing materials in key locations. Areas that can profit from soundproofing are bedrooms, bathrooms, workshops, and media rooms. To cut down on the amount of sound that flows into upper living areas and vice versa, it's a good idea to soundproof the basement ceiling as well as the walls.

There are a number of soundproofing materials you can use. Special fiberglass sound insulation batts fit into standard 2x4 wall cavities. They have paper backing on one side so they can easily be stapled to the surface of the studs. Doubling up on drywall layers is another way to reduce sound transmission – stagger the joints so they don't line up. Another technique involves using resilient channels to install the drywall. The channels hold the drywall away from the framing, which helps block the transmission of sound vibrations from one space to another.

Insulate drainpipes with soundproofing insulation. This will cut down on noise when people use the bathrooms. It's especially important with plastic pipes – plastic is noisier than cast iron.

Install a vapor barrier over the insulation. The barrier prevents inside moisture from penetrating and rotting the framing and insulation. Staple the vapor barrier to the studs. Overlap the plastic at the seams.

Install fiberglass soundproofing insulation on interior walls to reduce sound transmission from one room to another. Staple the kraft paper flanges to the stud faces.

Rigid foam furring

Rigid foam furring systems let you combine the jobs of installing furring and insulation into one process. The edges of the panels are grooved to accept 1x4 furring strips. To install the furring, hold the foam to the wall, position a 1x4 in the grooved edges of the panels, and secure it with masonry screws. Be sure to predrill; a drill/drive bit makes the job go a little faster.

Hanging Drywall

When hanging drywall, start with the ceiling. Fasten the perimeter of each sheet first, holding the fasteners back about ³⁄₈ inch from the edges so you don't damage them. Then remove the lift or T-braces, and finish attaching the sheet to the joists. You could wait until all the ceiling panels are up before putting the fasteners in the middle, but that makes it easier to lose sight of where the joists are.

Usually, drywall is installed so the long edges run perpendicular to the framing. Make sure to line up the joints correctly – the long tapered edges make shallow troughs that let you create almost invisible seams. Butt factory edges to factory edges and try to bury cut edges in corners.

When working on the walls, start at the top and work down. You'll probably find that it takes two people to raise a sheet of drywall

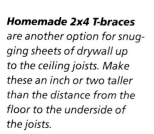

A drywall lift might be worth renting when dry-walling a ceiling. You place a piece of drywall facedown on the lift, crank it up to the ceiling, then nail or screw it to the joists.

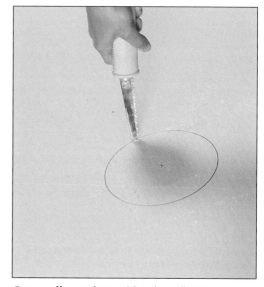

Cut small openings with a drywall utility saw. Make larger openings with a circle cutter. Smooth rough edges with a drywall rasp or surface-forming tool.

Homemade 2x4 T-braces are another option for snugging sheets of drywall up to the ceiling joists. Make these an inch or two taller than the distance from the floor to the underside of the joists.

Make straight cuts with a utility knife and a drywall T-square or a long straightedge. Prop the drywall sheet upright with the face toward you. Place the square on the drywall edge, then run a utility knife down the side of the square to score the cut. Snap the sheet along the score mark.

into position, snug it up to the ceiling, and drive in the nails. The job will be a little bit easier if you start nails across the top of these sheets before lifting them.

Space nails or screws no more than 6 inches apart along each ceiling joist and 8 inches apart along each stud. For ½-inch drywall, use 1¼-inch drywall nails or 1¼-inch drywall screws. For ⅝-inch drywall, use 1⅜-inch drywall nails or 1⅝-inch screws.

Make sure each fastener hits the framing. Any fastener that misses needs to be pulled out and the hole filled with joint compound. If you leave fasteners that miss the framing, they'll pop out someday.

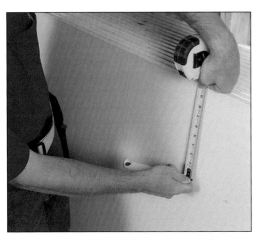

To keep long cuts straight, *measure and cut at the same time. Lock the tape measure to the dimension you want. Then, holding the tape measure along the top edge of the sheet and the utility knife against the tape hook, slide the tape measure along the sheet of drywall, scoring the drywall with the blade as you go.*

After scoring the sheet, *snap it in two, then cut through the paper backing with a utility knife. Smooth the cut edge with a drywall rasp.*

To cut inside corners for doorways, *fasten the sheet to the framing, then cut it to shape with a drywall saw.*

Use a drywall foot lift *to hold the bottom piece of drywall snug against the sheet above it. You just step on one side of the lifter and it raises the sheet up. A pry bar will work, too.*

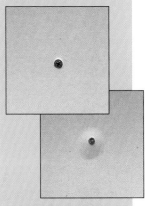

Taping and Mudding

The finishing process has several steps, each one taking you nearer to your goal of smooth, even walls. As with hanging drywall, tape and mud the ceiling first, then do the walls.

Before you start, make sure that all nail or screw heads are sunk below the surface of the drywall. Run a taping knife over them – you'll hear high fasteners click against the blade. In addition, double-check that you've installed corner bead on all the outside corners.

Joint compound comes either powdered or premixed. All-purpose premixed joint compound is generally a good choice and it's easy to use. Just don't stir it too much – you might wind up with air bubbles on the wall.

To get the joint tape to stick in the tape coat, tap it down in the center of the joint with your finger, then flatten it with the knife, working from the center to the ends with firm pressure. A thin layer of joint compound goes on top of the tape.

For the tape coat, *spread joint compound over the seam with a broad knife, press the tape into the mud, then load up the broad knife with a little more mud and embed the tape.*

A drywall finishing job *starts with the tape coat, where you apply joint compound and paper tape to the seams. From there the walls get a fill coat and a finish coat. While the tape coat levels off the wall, the fill and finish coats make the surface smooth.*

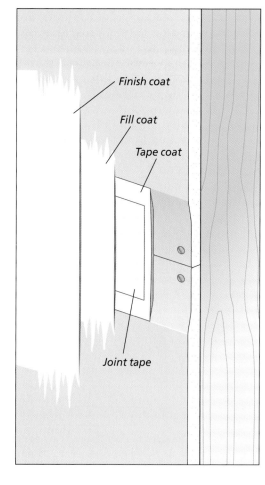

Finish coat

Fill coat

Tape coat

Joint tape

On inside corners, *thinly spread some joint compound, press in the prefolded tape, then run the knife down each side to embed the tape.*

On outside corners, *run joint compound down each side of the corner bead, holding the knife at a 45-degree angle. You want to cover the small dip between the metal corner ridge and the drywall surface.*

Coating screw and nail heads with joint compound is the last step in the tape coat. Fill each one, then level the whole row with one pass.

When working the fill coat, build the joints up a little in the middle and then feather them out smoothly. Use a stroke down each side, then one down the middle. You shouldn't be able to see the joint tape after completing the fill coat.

Let the tape coat dry at least overnight. When you start on the fill coat, use an 8- to 10-inch taping knife so you can feather out the mud on both sides of the joint. For the finish coat, use a 12- to 14-inch knife. The finish coat is worked the same as the fill coat; it's critical to feather the joints as smoothly as possible. Note that inside corners end up with only two coats of mud. Do one side of all the inside corners when you apply the fill coat, then do the other side when applying the finish coat.

Sand the joints after the finish coat has dried. No matter how careful you were with the finish coat, there will be a few stray ridges to get rid of. Be sure to wear a dust respirator. To confine the dust, cover entryways that lead to finished areas with plastic and turn off the furnace fan.

Applying texture

Because it's difficult to work on ceilings and a challenge to get them perfectly smooth, and because reflected light draws attention to any imperfections, ceilings are often textured. Perhaps the most common texture is a cottage-cheese effect, achieved by spraying on compound containing small bits of perlite.

Another approach is to apply plain texturing compound with a sprayer, then manipulate it with a scraper to create a knockdown finish. You can get different effects by rolling or troweling on the material instead. You can even swirl the material or create other patterns with a stiff brush.

No matter which texture you choose, it's best to do a trial run on a scrap piece of drywall first. Be sure to test the pressure on your sprayer and the consistency of your texture compound. If the compound leaves tiny spatters, thicken it a little to get the look you like.

For knockdown texture, use a rented sprayer to spray thinned joint compound onto the ceiling. You can also buy commercial texturing compounds made specifically for ceilings.

Let the compound set up for a few minutes, then flatten the surface with a squeegee-like knockdown knife. Figure out the set-up time and your knockdown technique during a test run.

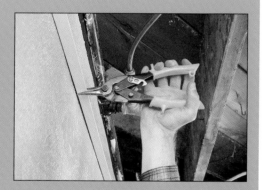

1 ***Determine the best ceiling height*** *for your situation and snap a level line around the perimeter of the room at that height. Nail the wall molding into studs along the chalk line.*

Suspended Ceilings

If there's enough headroom in the basement, a suspended ceiling is a good option. Essentially, a suspended ceiling is constructed of a metal grid that contains lightweight acoustical panels. The grid hangs from short wires attached to the ceiling joists, and below normal basement obstructions such as pipes and ductwork. And, since the acoustical panels can be popped out of the grid at any time, you can still easily access mechanical systems if you need to.

Suspended ceilings usually come with 2x2 or 2x4 acoustical panels in a variety of materials, colors, and patterns. Depending on the

2 ***Cut the main runners to length*** *and roughly position them on the molding. Starting at one side of the room, stretch a string line along the first main runner to make sure it's straight. Determine the length of each cross runner (they may vary slightly in length), then cut and install the cross runners.*

Compensating for wavy walls

Few walls are perfectly flat. You'll know yours aren't when you hold a piece of wall molding against the wall and see a dip or two behind it. Fortunately, you can make the molding conform to the wall so the dips aren't obvious.

Snug the molding to the wall with nail staples (left). Pound one leg into the wall behind the drywall and the other leg across the wall molding flange.

If you're dealing with a deep depression, the horizontal flange of the wall molding may buckle. To flatten it out again, snip it with aviation snips (right) and then staple the molding to the wall.

3 ***Insert screw eyes*** *(or the hardware provided by the manufacturer) into the joists and run a piece of wire from the screw eye to the main runner. This will be easier to do if you install a few cross runners to help hold the main runners in position. Make sure not to pull the assembly out of level.*

type of system you use, the runners that support the panels can be exposed, recessed, or hidden by the panels.

Installation

Installing a suspended ceiling starts with a good layout. Find the centerpoint of each wall, then lay out ceiling panels from there to the corners to see the size of the panels along the edges of the room. Ideally, you want to wind up with a balanced layout where cut panels (if needed) are of equal width at both ends of the ceiling. The border panels should be at least half the width of the uncut panels. If they're not, shift the layout over half a panel.

When you have the layout figured out, snap level lines around the room at the

4 **Install the cross runners** between the main runners. On the wall side they slip in place between the wall molding and the main runners. Measure both diagonals of the section to make sure the grid is square.

5 **If the slots aren't perfectly aligned** from one main runner to the next, you get parallelograms instead of squares. Just snip some material off one end of the runner to bring the cross runners back into alignment.

Boxing in a window

Sometimes you'll have to box out the ceiling around obstructions, such as pipes, ductwork, or windows. When you're drawing up your plans, account for any boxes – you'll need to buy extra materials and sometimes even order special pieces, depending on the installation.

Runner material can be notched and bent to form ribs around the obstruction, and then connected with pieces of wall molding. From there, it's a matter of filling in between with panels. These boxes hang from U-shaped channel molding that is riveted to the runners.

1 **To box out a window,** first nail wall molding where the box will meet the window casing. The wall molding will support the runners and panels. Before bending the molding, cut the flange that rests against the casing. Note the piece that extends past the casing – it will meet the edge molding on the wall.

2 **Use aluminum fascia** to make the sides of the box. To bend the fascia to a 90-degree angle, cut a notch in the flange with aviation snips then bend the fascia over a straightedge.

4 **Slide in the edge** molding then fasten it to the fascia above the panel so the fastener won't be visible. Always wear a dust respirator when handling or adjusting panels – some fibers will inevitably become airborne.

3 **Set the box in place** on the molding and runners. To attach the fascia to the grid, drill a pilot hole through the flange and grid piece and fasten with a machine screw or a pop rivet.

height you want the new ceiling. Make sure they're the same height on each wall or the ceiling will slope. Then nail the wall molding (which supports the ends of the main runners) to the walls along the chalk lines. As you build the grid, check it for square by measuring both diagonals in a grid section. If the section is square, the measurements will be exactly the same. You can also place your eye as close as possible to a cross runner and look across the room. If the cross runners aren't straight, adjust the appropriate main runner by trimming one of its ends.

Light fixtures

You need to plan where your lights will go before you lay out the ceiling grid. Either fluorescent or incandescent fixtures can be used in a suspended ceiling. Fluorescents are typically sold panel size. Incandescent fixtures can be inset into holes cut into the ceiling panels, but they have to be attached to the grid in some manner so their weight will be supported. Some models come with mounting hardware, others don't. Consult the manufacturer of your suspended ceiling for recommendations on lighting fixtures.

6 **Install the light fixture** by slipping it up through the grid then setting it in place. You might have to remove a cross runner or two to get the fixture in.

7 **Cut ceiling panels** faceup. Change blades frequently to keep cuts clean. Always wear a dust respirator when cutting and installing panels.

8 **Raise the ceiling panels** through the opening at an angle, then set them in place on the runners. To avoid smudging the panels, wash your hands frequently when handling the panels.

9 **The rest of the job** goes quickly. Be sure to store a few extra panels in a clean dry area in case you need to replace any later.

Good-looking floors go a long way *toward making basement rooms comfortable and enjoyable to use. There are flooring options available to fit most tastes and budgets – carpet, engineered wood, plastic-laminate, ceramic tile, and vinyl flooring are all suitable. Hardwood flooring is never recommended for use below grade because of possible moisture-related problems. Pick your flooring material early on, because the type of material can affect baseboard and door trim installation.*

Slab Preparation

Ceramic tile, carpet, vinyl, and some types of engineered wood and plastic-laminate flooring can be laid directly over a concrete slab, as long as the slab is in good condition. Consider framing a wooden subfloor (p. 52) if the slab is in poor condition or if you want the extra insulation.

When laying flooring directly over concrete, any unevenness in the slab will translate into wavy – and eventually damaged – finish flooring. To patch holes and cracks or to fill low spots, you can use either patching mortar or a latex patching compound. The benefit of the compound is that it cures more quickly

Clean the slab thoroughly *before you start installing the flooring. Scrape off dried joint compound, flaking paint, or any other stubborn debris with a floor scraper.*

Find any low spots *with a level. A strong light set on the floor helps highlight gaps under the level. Mark the outline of the dip with chalk or a pencil.*

than the mortar, but it's also more expensive. If the slab is riddled with low spots, cracks, and holes, you may be best off covering the entire floor with a self-leveling floor compound. Follow the directions on the package. Bear in mind that although they're called self-leveling, few products are – most require smoothing with a trowel. Dirty floors should be washed with a degreaser so that the adhesive can achieve an adequate bond. As a last step in preparing the slab, vacuum the surface thoroughly to eliminate concrete dust, which could interfere with the performance of the floor adhesive.

Trowel latex patching compound *into low spots and smooth it so the repair is flush with the surrounding floor surface.*

Knock high spots off *the slab with a cold chisel. Wear safety glasses to protect your eyes from flying concrete chips.*

Installing Carpet

First you need to decide which type of carpet to install. Cushion-backed carpet comes with the pad attached to the carpet. It's less expensive than standard carpet and pad, but there are fewer design and color choices available. Cushion-backed carpet is glued or taped to the slab and can be installed by a do-it-yourselfer.

Installation of either type of carpet starts with layout. Because carpet rolls typically measure 12 feet wide, you need to calculate how to orient the carpet so you don't have to seam it or, if seams are needed, where to place them so they're not in high-traffic areas or in conspicuous parts of the room. Think about which way the nap of the carpet will run. When you rub your hand against the pile, the fibers will ruffle, giving the carpet a shaded look. Make sure all pieces of carpet are installed with the nap going in the same direction.

Leave stretching to a pro

Standard carpet is installed over a separate pad and held in place by tackless strips (pieces of wood with protruding tacks that must be nailed into the concrete with masonry nails). This is a job best left to a professional installer.

Standard carpet must be evenly stretched or it can wrinkle, bubble, and wear out faster. Even though a piece of carpet is cut to fit the room, it still has a lot of slack in the middle that needs to be taken up. To do this the installer uses both a power stretcher and a knee kicker. While the tools aren't hard to use, it does take some skill to get the carpet perfectly tight.

Installing cushion-backed carpet

Install cushion-backed carpet with about 3 inches extra on all sides. Adhere it to the slab with all-purpose latex adhesive spread evenly over the concrete with a trowel. (Double-faced carpet tape can also be used. It doesn't hold as well as adhesive, but it makes it easier to remove the carpet for future replacement.) When the adhesive gets tacky, position the carpet and set it into the adhesive. Work a piece of 2x4 across the carpet to eliminate bumps and air bubbles. Finally, trim the carpet flush to the walls with a carpet knife.

The power stretcher is used to stretch carpet across the room. The power stretcher is braced and then extended across the room. The head has spikes that grab the carpet. When the lever on its side is pressed, the head moves forward, stretching the carpet.

The knee kicker is used to stretch the carpet near the wall and in small confined areas. The spiked head of the knee kicker is positioned near the edge of the carpet, then the installer kicks the padded end with his knee to push the tool forward and stretch the carpet.

The excess carpet is trimmed off after the carpet is stretched. The carpet trimmer has an offset guide that runs along the wall to guide the cut. A stair tool is used to tuck the carpet edge under the baseboard; it has a blunt edge so it won't cut the carpet fibers.

Out, damned spot

Unless you've banned people, pets, food, and beverage from your newly finished basement, it's only a matter of time until you'll be cleaning up the first spill on the carpet. Here's the basic plan of attack: For solids, scoop up as much as possible with a spoon. For liquids, blot – don't rub – with clean white rags or paper towels. Now apply warm (not hot) water to the stained area and blot it up with more clean rags or paper towels until they come away clean.

If a stain remains, mix a teaspoon of mild detergent with a quart of warm water and apply it with a clean rag. Leave it on for five minutes, then blot it up with more clean white rags. Rinse the area with warm water and blot up the excess. Continue to rinse and blot until the detergent is gone. Let the area dry before you vacuum it.

Wood and Wood-Look Floors

While solid wood flooring is not an option for a below-grade installation, you can install engineered-wood flooring. Another option is plastic-laminate flooring that looks like wood. Plastic-laminate flooring is installed as a floating floor; the planks are glued to each other along the edges, but the flooring is not attached to the underlayment at all. Engineered wood flooring can be glued down, stapled to a wood subfloor, or floated. Check the manufacturer's installation instructions to see which options are available for the flooring you choose.

Installing floating floors

Floating floors are usually installed over a thin foam underlayment. The floor can be made softer and quieter by installing a layer of fiberboard instead of foam underlayment. The fiberboard (also called carpet board) provides an impact-absorbing layer, much like carpet padding. Check the manufacturer's specifications to see if this is an option for your flooring.

2 *Dry-fit* the first three rows, glue them together, and let the glue cure. Strap clamps can be used in place of a tapping block to snug up the fit. Spacers between the wall and the first row of flooring allow for expansion and contraction.

4 *Tap the pieces* together, protecting the edge of the flooring with a tapping block. Never hit the edge of an unprotected plank or you'll damage the tongue. Wipe off excess glue with a damp rag.

1 *Moisture-proof the installation* by covering the concrete slab with 6-mil plastic sheeting. Overlap the seams by about 8 inches, then install an underlayment of either fiberboard or foam pad.

3 *Apply glue* along the entire length of the groove in each plank, then attach the board to the tongue in the adjacent plank. Be generous – as a rule of thumb, a pint of glue should cover about 100 square feet of flooring.

After installing a moisture barrier and the underlayment, dry-fit the first row of planks along the wall; the tongues should stick out into the room. If the wall is wavy or irregular, scribe the planks with a compass then trim them to shape with a jigsaw. Slip ¼-inch spacers between the walls and the planks, and leave the spacers in until all the flooring is laid. The gaps allow the flooring to expand; they will eventually be hidden by the baseboard.

Dry-fit the second and third rows of flooring, then carefully separate the planks and apply glue to the grooves in the ends of the planks in the first row. As you pull the joints closed, glue should ooze out – if it doesn't, use more. When gluing the second and third rows, apply glue to the grooves in both the ends and edges of the planks. Set each one in place and close the joints a hammer and tapping block or with clamp straps. Wipe up the glue and check that the planks are locked together. After gluing the planks in the second and third rows, wait an hour for the glue to cure before proceeding.

You'll have to cut planks to fit at walls and around obstacles. You can use a jigsaw with a fine-toothed blade, a circular saw with a thin-kerf carbide-tipped blade, or a handsaw. If you use a jigsaw or circular saw, place the plank facedown to avoid chipping the laminate surface; when using a handsaw, position the plank faceup.

When you get to the last row of planks, you'll probably have to rip them down to size with a circular saw.

Installing glue-down floors

In addition to being floated, engineered-wood floors can also be glued directly to a concrete slab with a water-based adhesive. Typically, manufacturers recommend that planks over 3 inches wide be glued down; narrower planks can be stapled to a wood subfloor.

The biggest issue with a glue-down floor is moisture. The concrete has to be dry or the glue won't hold and the wood could deform. Manufacturers recommend that you test for moisture before proceeding; follow the instructions that come with the flooring and adhesive you'll be using. In addition, the concrete surface must be perfectly clean to allow the glue to bond. Never use a concrete sealer before gluing.

Install the flooring parallel to the room's longest wall. Leave a ¼-inch gap for expansion and contraction between the flooring and the walls. Spread the adhesive in manageable sections, holding the trowel at a 45-degree angle. Let it set up according to the directions on the adhesive's label, insert a tongue of one plank into the groove of the neighboring plank, and drop the plank into position. Try not to slide the planks as you install them because this could disturb the bond. If the edges of the planks pull up after installation, weight them down with heavy objects. Stay off the floor for at least 24 hours after installation.

5 *Use a pull bar* anywhere you can't fit the tapping block and hammer. You'll need to use the pull bar with the end plank of each row.

Apply water-based adhesive with the trowel recommended by the manufacturer (usually a V-notched trowel). Water-based adhesives begin to cure quickly – only apply as much adhesive as you can cover in 30 minutes.

Join the tongue and groove edges of the planks then lower the plank into the adhesive – don't slide the flooring into the glue. If the joint isn't tight, use a hammer and tapping block to close the gap. Start the installation in a corner and work toward an exit so you don't have to walk on the floor before the adhesive has set.

Sheet Vinyl

Sheet vinyl is installed in one of two ways: fully adhered with adhesive spread over the entire underlayment, or perimeter bonded with adhesive spread only under the seam and edges of the flooring. Perimeter bonded vinyl is easier to install and will hide small imperfections in the underlayment. Fully adhered vinyl, on the other hand, is less likely to bubble, stretch, or tear. If the vinyl has to be seamed, the seam is cut and glued first with perimeter bonded vinyl; seams in fully adhered vinyl are cut and glued down after the rest of the flooring.

Preparing the slab

Surface preparation is the most important step in the process of installing sheet vinyl. Any bumps in the slab will telegraph through the flooring; any dips or low spots will eventually

Use a floor edger to *remove loose or chipping paint from the slab. When you rent the sander, ask what grit will be best for the work you need to do. Wear eye and ear protection and a particulate respirator.*

cause the flooring to crack. Grind off high spots with a grinder or knock them off with a hammer and chisel. If there's a coating of paint on the floor, rough it up with a sander. Make any necessary slab repairs (see pp. 23, 66).

Making the template

It's easiest to cut sheet vinyl to size in a room larger than the room in which you'll be installing it (a garage works well, provided it's dry, the weather is warm, and the floor is clean so dirt and gravel don't embed in the backing). First, make a template of the room where the vinyl will be installed. Use a heavy paper such as kraft paper or rosin paper. Lay sheets of paper over the floor to within an inch of the wall all around the room. Tape them together, then cut 3-inch-long ovals in the paper. Use these to tape the paper to the floor so the template won't slip while marking. Next set the leg of a framing square against the wall and position a pencil along the other edge of the leg. Slide the square and the pencil along the walls to draw a continuous line around the room. Ignore obstructions such as pipes.

Cutting the vinyl

If you have to make a seam, do that now. If the flooring has a tile pattern, the grout joint makes a natural seam. Lap one piece of vinyl

1 ***Make a template*** *by taping together sheets of heavy paper such as rosin or kraft paper. Mark the template by sliding one edge of a framing square along the walls of the room while marking a pencil line along the opposite edge.*

2 ***To cut the vinyl,*** *hold one edge of the leg of the same carpenter's square against the pencil line on the template and use the other side of the leg as a straightedge to cut the vinyl. Make sure to hold the blade perfectly vertical.*

over the other, making sure to match the pattern along the entire length of the seam. When the pieces are perfectly aligned, tape them together. Position the template over the vinyl and tape it through the ovals to keep it from slipping. Use the same framing square you used to mark the template as a straightedge while you cut the vinyl.

Positioning the vinyl

Move the vinyl into the room where you're going to install it and position it on the floor.

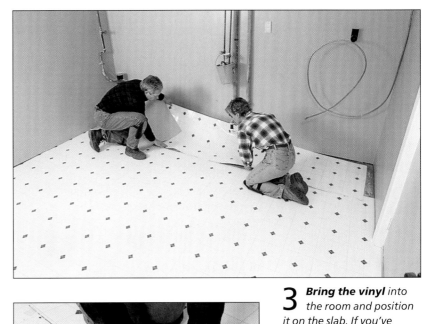

3 **Bring the vinyl** into the room and position it on the slab. If you've moved the flooring in two separate pieces, realign the seam.

4 **Trim around large obstacles** such as floor drains. Note the spiral cut; by starting in the middle and working outward, you can see where you're going and get a clean cut on exposed edges.

5 **Cut the seam** with a utility knife using a straightedge to guide the cut. Hold the blade perfectly vertical. Remove the scraps then fold each piece away from the seam.

6 **Spread adhesive** with a notched trowel. You should spread the adhesive several inches along each side of the seam and a foot or two out from the walls at each end of the seam.

7 **Lay the flooring** in place, carefully aligning the seam. Note how the adhesive has been applied around the perimeter of the area to be covered by the flooring piece; this works fine with smaller pieces. With larger pieces of vinyl, it's best to do the seam first, then the edges.

8 ***Carefully roll*** *the vinyl to set it firmly into the adhesive and to remove air bubbles. Use a small J-roller if you have one or rent a heavier version such as the one seen here.*

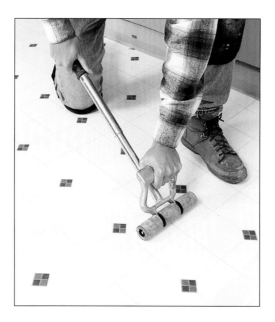

9 ***Seal the edges*** *of the vinyl. Apply a seam sealer in the seam and caulk around the edges of the room and around any obstructions.*

Retape the seam if necessary, then cut through the overlapping material with a utility knife and fresh blade. For the least visible seam, cut along the edge of a grout line, not the center. Trim the vinyl roughly to size around any obstacles – you'll trim it precisely after you've glued down the vinyl.

Gluing perimeter bond vinyl

When installing vinyl flooring, always use the adhesive recommended by the manufacturer and follow their directions, or you may void the warranty. Some manufacturers include tracers in the adhesive; if the adhesive is analyzed because of a floor failure issue and the correct tracers aren't present, the warranty won't apply.

Apply adhesive under the seam first. Lay both pieces of the flooring in the adhesive, match up the seam, and roll out any air bubbles. Now carefully pull the flooring back from the wall in one half of the room and apply adhesive along the edges of the floor. Gently lay the vinyl back down, one corner at a time, pressing it down as flat as possible. Trim the vinyl around any obstructions and roll it into the adhesive with a J-roller. Repeat the process with the vinyl on the other side of the room.

Installing vinyl tiles

Vinyl tiles are easy to install but the floor must be smooth, clean, and in good condition. You can use self-stick tiles or dry-back tiles which are embedded in floor adhesive. Both are laid out along chalk lines snapped across the center of the room. The tiles are set one quadrant at a time, starting from the intersection of the guide lines and working out in a reverse pyramid. After the tiles are set, the entire floor should be rolled with a 100-pound roller to force out any air bubbles.

Set the tiles in one quadrant at a time. Start at the intersection of the chalk lines and work back and forth between the lines. Drop the tiles into place rather than sliding them.

To mark a tile for cutting, *set the tile to be cut on top of the last full tile. Use a third tile as a marking gauge – slide it all the way to the wall and mark along its edge.*

BATHROOM FINISHING

Putting the finishing touches on a bathroom is satisfying work because that's when you really start to see the results of your hard work. At this stage you finish off wall and floor surfaces and install the cabinets and the countertop. You also install the sink and shower fixtures and do the final electrical hookups.

Ceramic Tile Tub Surround

To prevent eventual moisture damage, tiles in wet areas should be set on an underlayment of cement backer board. The adhesive you'll be using to set the tiles will dictate how the backer board is installed: smooth side out with mastic, rough side out with thinset. Although professional tilesetters use thinset to set wall tiles in wet areas, we prefer to use mastic. Mastic grabs the tiles right away so they aren't likely to slide down the wall.

1 ***Tape the seams*** *between backer board panels with fiberglass mesh tape. Lightly press it into the thinset with your fingers then embed it with a broad knife.*

2 ***Mark layout lines*** *on the back wall. The horizontal and vertical layout lines must be absolutely perpendicular – if they're not, the whole layout will be off.*

3 ***To test your layout,*** *rest a piece of straight 1x4 on the edge of the tub and position the tiles. Begin at the centerline and work toward the ends.*

4 ***Spread adhesive*** *with the straight edge of the trowel, then comb it into ridges with the notched edge. Work in small areas so you have time to set and adjust the tile before the mastic skins over.*

5 ***Push grout into the joints*** *between tiles with a grout float – hold it at about a 30-degree angle. Then hold the float on edge and scrape as much excess grout off the tiles as possible. Wipe off the remaining grout with a clean damp sponge. After the grout has begun to set up, polish off the haze with cheesecloth.*

Install the backer board panels from the bottom of the wall up, leaving about ⅛ inch of space between panels and ¼ inch between the backer board and the tub edge. Fasten the panels to the studs with 1½-inch galvanized roofing nails or 1¼- or 1⅝-inch backer board screws spaced every 8 inches. Fill the joints between panels with thinset adhesive, tape them with fiberglass backer board tape, then level the joints with a broad knife.

Layout

Start with the back wall of the surround. Find the high spot of the tub, then measure up one tile plus ¼ inch and make a horizontal line there. Next draw a vertical line down the center of the wall. The two lines must be absolutely perpendicular. Now set out some tiles from the centerline over to the edge of the wall and see what size the cut tile at the edge will be (cut tiles more than half a tile wide look best). Avoid cut tiles narrower than a half-tile wide because they're unattractive and hard to set. If necessary, juggle the layout to get wider tiles. For example, if you started out with a grout joint centered on the vertical line, shift the layout so that a tile is centered on the line instead. It helps to rest the tiles on a 1x4 laid along the tub edge while you're playing with the layout.

Plan on using full tiles at the outside edge (room side) of the end walls since this is the most visible part of the enclosure. If necessary, it's worth the compromise of putting narrow cuts at the inside corner where the end walls meet the back wall.

If you won't be installing tile right up to the ceiling, draw horizontal lines on all the tub walls to mark where the tiles will end so you won't get adhesive on drywall that will be painted. As a last step, mark for accessories, such as soap dishes and towel bars.

Installation

Spread and comb the mastic with the trowel specified by the adhesive manufacturer. V-notched trowels are usually used with mastics, but recommendations vary. Don't put adhesive on the areas where accessories will be mounted.

Start setting tile at the bottom of the back wall at the intersection of your reference lines, and work out toward the edges. Align each tile and press it into the adhesive. After finishing the back wall, move on to the end walls.

Fiberglass Tub Surround

While tub surround kits fit most tubs exactly, the panels can be trimmed with aviation snips if necessary. Make the cut at an inside corner where molding will eventually cover the cut edge. You'll also have to cut holes for faucets and a showerhead in the panel that will go at the head of the tub. Once the panels are cut, apply adhesive to the walls with a caulk gun (follow the manufacturer's directions to the letter – they can vary from manufacturer to manufacturer) and press the panels in place, leaving a ¼-inch gap between the top edge of the tub and the bottom of the panels. Put in the corner moldings and brace the surround until the adhesive cures, usually about 24 hours. Finally, caulk around the fittings, along the top of the tub, and along the moldings.

1 *Make a cardboard template of the wet wall and use it to transfer the location of the plumbing stub-outs to the end wall panel.*

2 *For large holes, bore a starter hole with a drill then cut the opening with a jigsaw. For smaller holes you can use a hole saw or a spade bit. Cut all holes with the panel faceup.*

3 *Brace the panels with scrap 2x4s until the adhesive has cured. Use a combination of different-sized pieces to bridge contours in the panels.*

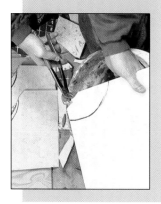

Ceramic Tile Floor

Y̶ou can set tile directly on the slab, provided it's clean, in good shape, and perfectly even. If the slab has small cracks in it, spread an isolation membrane before tiling.

Layout

With floors, the first goal of layout is to find the arrangement of tiles that looks best in the room. The second goal is to divide the floor into working sections with straight and square lines, so that all the tiles will line up when you set them. Start by snapping a chalk line perpendicular to the focal point of the room, then dry-lay a row or two of tiles to see where the last full tiles will fall. Adjust the tile layout so that the cut tiles are at least half as wide as the full tiles. Then snap a line perpendicular to the first line. Dry-lay the tiles along this line to check the layout. You may have to juggle both lines to get a layout you like. Once you like the look of the layout, snap lines to make a grid with sections sized to contain full tiles plus the grout joints between them.

Setting floor tiles

Use thinset mortar to set floor tiles (mastic can't support the weight that a floor bears).

Spread the thinset evenly with the straight edge of a square-notched trowel, then comb the thinset into uniform ridges with the notched side. Lay the tiles starting in a corner of the grid section. After you've finished setting the section, use a rubber mallet to tamp down any tiles that are sitting higher than the rest, then fine-tune the alignment of the tiles.

Once all the tiles are installed, let the thinset cure for 24 hours then grout the floor with sanded grout. Sanded grout is used for any grout joint that is wider than ⅛ inch. It is stronger than plain unsanded grout, which is used to fill joints narrower than ⅛ inch.

1 *Set each tile* then give it a slight twist to ensure good contact between the tile and adhesive. Work in 3- to 4-foot square sections.

2 *Matching cut tiles* frame this drainpipe. The fixture will cover the edges so it's okay to use nippers to make these cuts.

3 *A tile baseboard* caps off the floor. There are no trim tiles available for the tiles seen here; cut tiles placed with the rounded factory edge up fill in for the bullnose tiles available with many other lines of floor tile.

4 *Force grout into the joints* between tiles. Hold the float at about a 30-degree angle and make diagonal strokes to push the grout down into the joints.

Ceramic Tile Countertop

Make the underlayment for a ceramic tile countertop from ¾-inch exterior grade plywood topped with ½-inch backer board. First glue and screw the plywood to the cabinets and mark the sink opening using the manufacturer's template. Cut it out, then transfer the opening to the backer board by tracing the sink cutout from the plywood onto the backer board. You have to score the backer board on both sides in order to cut the sink opening. To make sure the score marks line up, drive nails through the backer board at several points along the first pencil line, then use the nail holes to position the template on the other side. Finally, secure the backer board to the plywood with thinset adhesive and screws or nails.

Countertop layout begins with the edge tiles. Adjust these back and forth until you have a balanced layout, then lay out tiles from the front of the counter to the back. If you have to use cut tiles, put them along the wall – not the front edge. Also check how the tiles will fit around the sink. When you have a layout you like, use a framing square to draw reference lines on the backer board.

Set the edge tiles first. Trowel thinset along the edge, then apply a thick bead of silicone adhesive behind the front face of the edge tile (silicone adhesive adheres to the plywood better than thinset does). Next set the counter tiles. Work in 2-foot sections, making sure all the tiles are at the same height and the grout joints are straight and even. Allow the thinset to cure for about 24 hours before grouting.

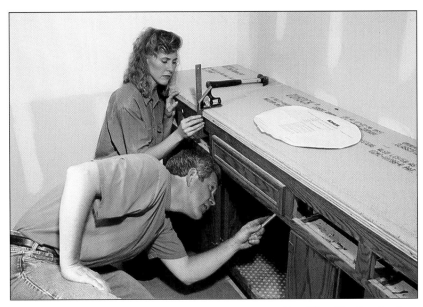

1 *Align the front edges* of the backer board and plywood, then reach inside the cabinet and trace the sink cutout from the plywood onto the backer board.

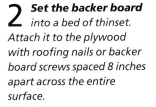

2 *Set the backer board* into a bed of thinset. Attach it to the plywood with roofing nails or backer board screws spaced 8 inches apart across the entire surface.

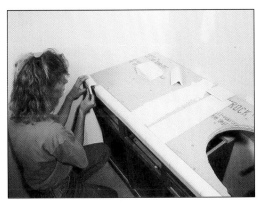

3 *Lay out the edge tiles first,* moving them back and forth until the cut pieces at the ends will be equal sized. Then lay out a few rows of counter tiles from the edge to the wall.

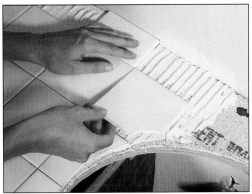

4 *Make curved cuts* with tile nippers. You'll break fewer tiles if you nibble away the excess in small bits. Nonetheless, expect to break a few tiles before the job is done.

1 Drill pilot holes, then drive 2½-inch screws through the hanging rail into each stud. Make sure the cabinet is level front to back along each side, and side to side across the front and rear.

2 Sand the backsplash to the pencil line with a belt sander after scribing it to the wall.

3 Attach the faucet, tailpiece, and stopper assembly to the sink before you set it in place. This will minimize the amount of time you have to spend under the sink in the cabinet.

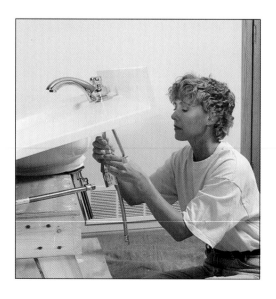

Cabinets and Countertops

Because few floors are level, begin your cabinet installation by finding and marking the highest point in the floor – you'll be shimming every cabinet to this height. Measure up from the high point, and mark the cabinet's top line with a level (standard kitchen cabinets are 34½ inches tall and standard vanity cabinets are 33½ inches tall).

Where you start installing cabinets depends on the area where you're installing them. If the cabinets are in an alcove and run wall to wall, measure to double-check that they fit, then start the installation with the sink cabinet. If the run of cabinets will abut a wall only on one end, start the installation with the corner cabinet.

Set the first cabinet in place and shim it to bring it up to the level line on the wall. Then fasten the cabinet to the studs. If there's a gap between the cabinet and the wall, insert a shim there before driving the screws or the cabinet will be pulled out of square.

If you're installing additional cabinets, shim the next one up to the level line on the wall and clamp both cabinets together. Screw the cabinets together through the face-frame stiles. Predrill for the screws, and try to position

4 A few dabs of silicone adhesive will hold the counter (this one has an integral sink) in place on the cabinet.

them so they'll be hidden behind the door hinges. Then screw the second cabinet to the wall studs.

Countertops

Plastic laminate is by far the most popular and affordable countertop material. You can special-order counters to exact length from a home center or buy them ready-made. Two styles are typically sold: square-edged counters with a separate backsplash and less expensive postformed tops that have an integral backsplash.

If you buy a ready-made counter, you'll have to cut it to fit your cabinets. Turn the counter upside down and cut it from the back side with a circular saw. If you're cutting a postformed counter, the saw won't be able to make it all the way through the backsplash, and you'll have to finish up with a handsaw or a jigsaw. Since plastic laminate tends to chip during cutting, cut the countertop ⅛ inch longer than needed, then sand it down to size with a belt sander. If your counter turns a corner, assemble the mitered corner joint before installing the counter. Insert the draw bolts into the prebored holes in the underside of the counters, run a thick bead of silicone caulk along the joint, then tighten the bolts to draw the seam closed.

Cultured marble and solid-surface counters are fairly easy to install. These are bonded to the cabinets with silicone adhesive.

Installing a laminate countertop

Lay a bead of adhesive on the cabinet top, slide the counter in at an angle with one end lifted in the air, then push down on the raised end. Drive screws up through the cabinet's corner blocks. The length of screw required depends on the distance from the corner block to the counter – make sure the screws aren't too long. To ensure that the counter is tight against the cabinets, have someone lean down on the counter as you drive each screw.

Install the backsplash next. Start by scribing the backsplash to match any irregularities in the wall. Set the backsplash against the wall, set a compass to the largest gap between the surface and the wall, then run the compass along the wall so that you're tracing the shape of the wall onto the surface. Then sand the backsplash to fit and attach it to the wall and the counter with two beads of adhesive caulk on the back of the backsplash and one bead on the counter.

Finish by cutting the sink opening. First drill a starter hole, then make the cut with a jigsaw. Put tape on the saw's baseplate to keep the saw from scratching the laminate.

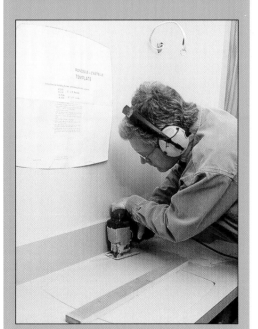

Cut the sink opening in a laminate counter-top with a jigsaw. After cutting the sides of the sink opening, fasten scrap lumber to the cutout to keep it from suddenly dropping out and chipping the laminate as you near the end of the cut.

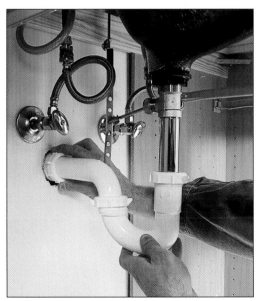

5 *To connect the sink trap,* slip the J-shaped piece onto the tailpiece and the L-shaped piece into the trap adapter. Align everything and tighten all the slip nuts.

Toilet and Electrical Trim-Out

Why level a toilet?

The relationship of the water surface to the bowl is an important part of the design of a 1.6 gallon toilet. The bowl must be level or it might not flush well. If necessary, use plastic shims to level the bowl and to prevent it from rocking, which could break the wax seal.

Level the tank as well. If both the tank and the bowl are level, you'll know that the hold-down bolts are equally tight and the gasket isn't going to leak.

Finish up the bathroom by installing the fixtures and making the final electrical connections. Almost everything you'll be working on at this point comes with instructions – read them, follow them, and work carefully so you don't damage the surfaces of the fittings and fixtures. To protect the finish, wrap a rag or a piece of chamois around the fitting you're installing, or wrap tape around the pliers jaws. Lay cardboard over the floor or the counter – whichever you're using as a work surface – to protect it.

To hook up switches and receptacles, strip ¾ inch of insulation from the wire ends. Bend each wire into a loop, then set it clockwise around the screw so it will be pulled tight as you tighten the screw. Attach the wires in order: ground, neutral, and then hot. Connect neutral leads to silver terminals and hot leads to brass terminals.

Connect the toilet shutoff. *Use two wrenches to tighten compression fittings. Later, you can use either a braided steel flexible line or chromed copper tubing to connect the toilet.*

Set the wax ring *onto the closet flange. Press down hard on the bowl to compress the ring. Then tighten the closet bolts – don't overtighten them or you could crack the bowl.*

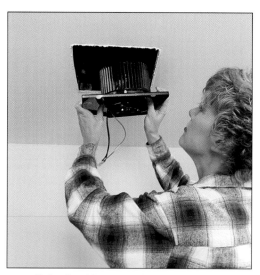

Install the fan blower *and make the final connections in the ceiling opening according to the manufacturer's instructions.*

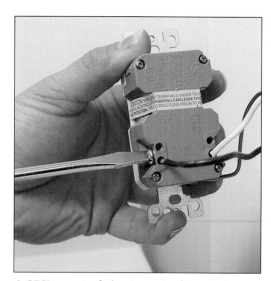

A GFCI receptacle *has two sets of terminals – one labeled line, the other, load. Incoming power goes to the line terminals. Connect outgoing wires to the load terminals. This provides protection to all the outlets downstream in the circuit.*

FINISHING UP

While you may be champing at the bit *to finish up all the little details that will make your basement livable, this is no time to rush. The attention you pay to the final stages of the project – including hanging doors and installing trim – will pay off big in the quality of the finished product. If shelves and cabinets were included in your plan, this is the time you'll attach them to the walls. You'll also be painting, staining, and varnishing during this part of the project.*

During these finishing stages, you'll also need to make the final connections at light fixtures, switches, and receptacles. If you've installed electric baseboard heat, you'll need to connect the baseboards, too.

Doors

When selecting an interior door, you can choose between prehung and unassembled varieties. Prehung doors are the easiest to install. They come hinged and hung on a fully assembled set of top and side jambs – some types even have trim, called casing, installed on one side of the jambs. The entire assembly pops into the opening and all you have to do is square the door with shims and fasten it in place. If you're replacing an existing door and the jambs are in good condition, you could buy a replacement door, called a door blank, which would save you from ripping out the old door jambs. However, you'll have to mortise it to accept the hinges, which can be tricky, and bore the door for the handle. You'll also need to mortise the jambs for the hinges and strike plate.

You can also choose among three types of construction: hollow- and solid-core, and solid-wood. Hollow-core doors have a cardboard baffle center covered by veneer. They're the least expensive doors you can buy. Solid-core doors are made of a wood composite core covered with wood veneer. They're more durable than hollow-core doors and won't warp or open up at the joints. Solid-wood doors are constructed entirely of wood and can be made with or without panel inserts. They're the most expensive type of door. Both solid-core and solid-wood doors are attractive and block sound transmission to some extent.

There's one more decision to make when you're door shopping: whether you want a flush or a panel door. Flush doors have a smooth surface and generally cost less than a panel door. Panel doors have inset pieces that give a more elaborate look. Personal taste and price often dictate what kind of door surface to choose.

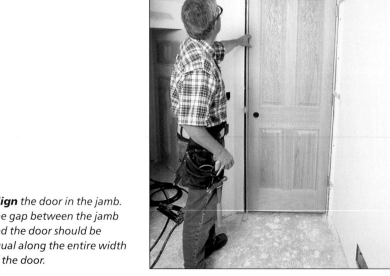

Shim between the door jamb and the rough opening using a carpenter's level to make sure that the jamb is perfectly plumb. Secure the hinge jamb in position with 8d finishing nails.

Align the door in the jamb. The gap between the jamb and the door should be equal along the entire width of the door.

Nail at stress points like hinges and latches. Make sure to shim between the jamb and the framing wherever you drive a nail. Pneumatic tools eliminate the need to drill pilot holes when nailing through the jamb and shims into the framing.

Installation tips

If you're installing a solid door, you may find that its weight makes it awkward to maneuver the door assembly when you're shimming it in the rough opening. Although many people leave the door in place, it's easier to plumb and secure the jambs with the door removed.

Start installing the jambs at the hinge side. Plumb the hinge jamb then nail it in place. Now you can rehang the door. With the door closed, adjust the jamb on the latch side until the gap between the top of the door and the head jamb is equal all the way across the top of the door, then secure the jamb to the framing.

When you nail the jambs in place, locate the nails at the stress points like the hinges and the latch. You should be able to place these nails so they'll be hidden by the hinges and strike plate. Be sure to fill the gap between the jambs and the framing with shims wherever you drive a nail.

All doors – especially heavy solid-core doors – need to be well anchored to the framing. At each hinge, use at least one screw that's long enough to go all the way into the stud.

If you'll be reusing a door and putting in new flooring, you may have to trim the bottom of the door. Hollow-core doors have a plug in the bottom. If you're trimming quite a bit, you may trim off the plug and expose the cavity. In that case, chisel the veneer off the plug and glue it back into the bottom of the door.

Bifold doors

Bifold doors are often used for closets and small utility rooms because they save space; since they fold together rather than swing out, you can place furniture right up to both sides of the closet opening. When open, bifold doors allow full access to the doorway, making them ideal doors to use for laundry or toy closets.

Follow the installation instructions that come with the door. Typically, the first task is to install the top track. Some doors may have a bottom track, but it's more usual for the hardware to consist of a single foot bracket on each side. (If the door has been framed at the wrong height, you might need to put a block under the foot bracket to gain height.) To install the door, insert the bottom pivot point, then tip the top pivot point into place. Position the sliding guides in the track and adjust the panels as necessary to space them evenly. To raise or lower the panels, adjust the height of the lower pivot pin.

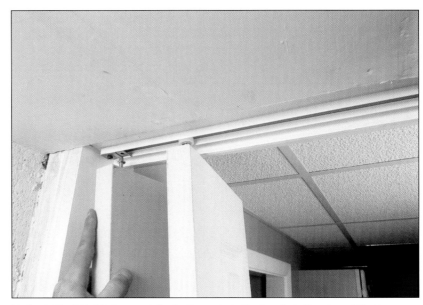

To install a bifold door, set the bottom pin in the bracket, then insert the top pivot pin in the socket in the top track. Hold down the top pivot – it's spring-loaded.

Trim a door to size with a circular saw. Place tape on the door to prevent the sawplate from scratching the finish. Before cutting, score the cut line with a utility knife to reduce the possibility of chipping the veneer.

Finish Carpentry

Moldings finish off a room and help hide any rough edges. Door and window casing conceals gaps between the wall and the jambs. Baseboard molding covers the gap between the walls and the floor and protects the bottom of the wall from shoes and vacuums. If your design calls for one, a finished ledge or shelf on top of a partial-height block wall provides useful storage space for books or other small items.

Miter joints

Miter joints are often used to join pieces of baseboard molding and window and door casing. It can be tricky to cut them accurately, but with practice, you'll be able to make a tight joint.

One thing that can throw off the fit is a surface that isn't perfectly flat. To compensate for this, back-bevel the cut by lifting the piece of trim just a little bit with a pencil or the small end of a shim when you cut it. Test-fit the trim before you install it, then glue the joint and nail through the joint in both directions.

Extension jambs

In basement remodeling it's common to have to fur out a wall to get around an obstruction such as a drain pipe, to add insulation, or just to finish the wall with drywall. Because the wall is now thicker than the window jamb, you'll need to extend the window jambs; order extension jambs when you order the window.

Finishing up

Use a nailset to sink all the nail heads below the surface. For a smooth surface, fill all the nail holes with wood putty. If you'll be painting the woodwork, fill the holes first. If you'll be staining the woodwork, fill the holes after you've stained the wood and applied a coat of sanding sealer.

1 *Finish ledges* with durable material such as wood or solid-surface material. Here we've built up the height of the ledge so that the window stool and the ledge are continuous.

2 *Wood biscuits* strengthen butt joints. Put wood glue in the slots before inserting the biscuits – the moisture in the glue swells the wood, locking the joint.

3 *Miter window casing* at the corner for a snug fit. Glue the joint together with wood glue, nail in both directions, then wipe off the excess glue. Note that the front edge of the ledge is finished with Princeton molding to hide the edge of the veneer plywood.

1 **Cope molding** that meets at inside corners. Miter the piece first, then use a coping saw to trim one piece of base to fit the profile of the mating piece.

2 **Test-fit the joint**. If small adjustments are needed, make them with a rat-tail file.

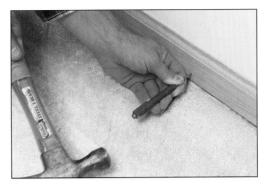

3 **Nail baseboards** to the studs, then set the nail heads slightly below the surface with a nail set. Prevent splits in hardwood molding by drilling pilot holes before nailing.

1 **Use wooden biscuits** to join the extensions to the window jambs. The closer the slots are placed together, the stronger the joint.

3 **Nail the window casing** to the jambs. If you're using a hammer and nails instead of a finish nailer, drill pilot holes in the casing first to avoid splitting.

2 **Fit the extension jambs** to the existing jambs. Then shim the sides straight and nail the extension jambs to the framing.

Biscuit joints

Use biscuits and a biscuit joiner to join planks edge to edge. The biscuit joiner has a retractable saw blade that cuts small slots. To make sure the slots match up, align the pieces of wood and make a mark across both pieces. Then use the lines to align the biscuit joiner before you cut the slots. To assemble the joint, apply glue to the slots and insert the biscuits. The biscuits are made of compressed beech wood. Moisture in the glue makes the biscuits swell to a tight fit – make any adjustments to the joint before the biscuit swells.

Shelves and Cabinets

Building a custom bookshelf is a lot like constructing a box. The ones shown here are made from ¾-inch oak veneer plywood with a ¼-inch plywood back. The raw plywood edges are hidden with a piece of solid oak molding.

When installing cabinets, refer often to the drawing that shows the size and placement of all the cabinets, filler strips, and other key components. Otherwise, it's easy to mix up the dozens of parts and pieces you'll be juggling. The cabinets used in this application are 29-inch units designed for home office use.

Attach a hardwood hanging rail to the back of the shelf unit. Screwing into the wall studs through both the hanging rail and the plywood is more secure than just screwing through the plywood alone.

Cover the raw edges of the plywood with molding such as the Princeton stop seen here.

Screw base cabinets to the wall studs through the hanging rail at the back of the cabinet after filling any gaps between the rail and the wall with shims.

Shim each cabinet as needed to make it plumb and level. The backs of these cabinets will be finished with matching plywood ordered from the cabinet manufacturer.

Stain, Varnish, and Paint

Protect any surfaces you don't want to stain, varnish, or paint with masking tape – but try the tape in an inconspicuous area first. All tapes are not created equal and the wrong one will pull the paper off the wall, creating unnecessary repair work.

When you apply stain, use a brush or a lambswool applicator. Applicators drip a lot less than brushes and, since you can load them up with more stain, you can spread the stain out over a larger area without reloading. After it dries, coat stained wood with a clear finish such as varnish or polyurethane. To avoid specks in the finish, don't apply a clear finish until all the dusty work is done, the dust has settled, and the area has been thoroughly vacuumed.

Always prime new drywall before you paint it. Drywall paper and joint compound have different textures and absorb moisture at different rates. If you paint without priming, the paint will look different over the drywall than it will over the joint compound. When priming and painting, start with the ceiling, then do the walls. As you go, use a paintbrush to cut in areas you can't paint with a roller, such as corners and around molding.

Roll on the paint as soon as you've finished cutting in the area. Keep a wet edge – for the best looking job, wet paint should overlap wet paint.

Apply stain, let it soak in for a minute, then wipe it off. If you're trying to match other stained woodwork, you'll have to figure out how long to let the stain soak in before you wipe it off. Leaving the stain on longer will result in a darker color.

Brush on a coat of sanding sealer, let it dry overnight, then sand off the raised grain before brushing on a coat of varnish. For all clear finishes, hold the brush at a 45-degree angle to the wood and work along the grain. Don't overlap strokes.

Cut in walls before painting them. Extend the paint far enough out so you can reach it with a roller. As soon as you've cut in an area, roll it out so the small band of paint doesn't dry before it can be blended into the paint of adjacent surfaces.

Roll on paint in a small W, then even it out using vertical strokes and lifting the roller at the end of every pass. Don't over-roll because the dry roller cover will start to pull the paint back off the wall.

Electrical Trim-Out

The main wiring for the basement was done when the mechanical systems were roughed-in. Wrapping up the electrical work at this stage of the job consists of all the small tasks that need to be done, such as hooking up fixtures, switches, receptacles, and appliances.

To strip wire ends, use a wire stripper or a multi-purpose tool. Strip off about an inch of the insulation. Loop the wire ends clockwise around screwheads so they tighten as the screws are tightened.

Recessed lights

If you've installed recessed lights, this is the time to attach the trim piece to the bottom of each fixture. Follow the manufacturer's instructions. Some trim pieces hook onto the housing with two springs; others clip on with long rigid wires.

If the trim won't sit flat to the ceiling, you can try these tricks. Some fixtures are made to work with either clips or springs. Even if the fixture is supplied with springs, it will still have clip holders. The clip holders can catch, so bend them out of the way if the trim is not sitting flush. Also, the springs may not be taut enough to pull up the trim. Loosen the wing nut, slide the fixture up a bit, then reinstall the trim.

Baseboard heaters

To install electric baseboard heaters, follow the schematic that comes with the heaters. In general, you'll be nailing or screwing the heater to at least two studs through mounting holes at the back of the baseboard housing. Then you'll remove the wiring compartment cover and make the connections. Heaters can be either 120 or 240 volts. When you're installing it, make sure to connect the heater to the matching power supply (for example, a 120-volt heater to a 120-volt power supply).

Finish installing recessed light fixtures by attaching the trim-kit rings following the manufacturer's instructions.

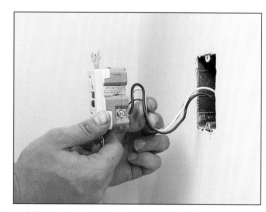

Folding leads accordion style makes it easier to fit them into the electrical box.

Connect baseboard heaters according to the manufacturer's schematic. Baseboard heaters are available in both 120-volt and 240-volt models, so make sure you've provided the proper circuit for your heater before you hook it up.

SPECIAL PROJECTS

Details such as a fireplace, wet bar, high-tech media equipment, or finished laundry room customize your living space and make a basement living area enjoyable to use. It's almost an unwritten rule that a few fun items should be included in a basement remodel. Keep these items and spaces in mind during the initial design phase – you'll have to pay attention to traffic flow around equipment and between rooms, and perhaps even add extra storage space. Sometimes special equipment can affect mechanical systems and framing, so make sure to factor this into your plans, too.

Gas Fireplace

For the easiest fireplace installation, choose a zero-clearance, direct-vent gas model. These don't require a chimney to vent exhaust gases or additional clearance where they meet combustible materials like wood framing or drywall. Still, it's important to check your local building code before installing a fireplace. You'll also need to contract with a plumber to run the gas line, and perhaps with an electrician to install the fan, remote switch, and other accessories.

Use the specifications that come with your fireplace to frame the space. If you want to raise the fireplace, add a plywood platform. Notice that the vent pipe has two walls: the inner pipe exhausts gases, while the outer pipe draws fresh air into the burner. You may have to purchase the pipe separately or add additional pieces.

You can finish around the fireplace with a number of materials ranging from stone to ceramic tile. We chose cast stone for this project. It's a man-made product with a flat, grooved back for adhering to mortar. It's light, easy to work with, and less expensive than

1 ***Slide the unit into place*** *after attaching the vent pipe and elbow. At the same time, fish the gas supply line through the opening. Follow the manufacturer's instructions for installing the vent.*

2 ***Connect the interlocking vent pipes*** *after securing the side flanges of the fireplace to the wall framing.*

3 ***To prepare*** *for a cast-stone surround, staple on metal lath and apply a scratch coat of mason's mix to the mesh using a steel concrete trowel and a mason's hawk. Then attach your mantel.*

real stone. For a rustic look, set the stone in a random pattern. To maintain the appearance of dry-laid field stone, keep the spaces between the stones as small as possible.

If you plan to install cabinets alongside the fireplace, the installation will look more realistic if you install the cabinets after the stone and scribe the cabinets' filler strips to conform to the stone. This is a complicated procedure that takes some skill. If you haven't done a lot of scribing, you'll find it easier to install the cabinets before the stone.

4 *Back-butter each stone* with a margin trowel and set it firmly in place. You'll get a better bond if you lay up the stone while the scratch coat is still wet. Space the stones so they're almost touching.

5 *Grout between the stones* with a grout bag filled with mason's mix. Smooth out the grout with your finger (wear rubber gloves). After the material sets up a bit, use a whisk broom to texture the grout and brush any excess off the stones.

6 *If you're setting a cabinet* right up to the stone, you'll have to attach a filler strip to the cabinet edge. Plumb it up tight to the stone, and scribe the profile onto the filler strip with a compass and pencil.

7 *Test-fit the filler strip* after cutting away the excess with a jigsaw. Fine-tune the fit with a narrow belt sander. Then check the cabinets for plumb and screw them to the wall framing.

8 *Arrange the decorative logs* and ash that come with the fireplace and make the final gas hookups using an approved connector. Brush soapy water on the connection and check for bubbles – a sure sign of a leak.

Wet Bar

Think carefully about how you will use a wet bar before you design it. Will it be used just for parties, or will your family treat it more like a mini kitchen? If the latter, you'll want more storage space, a small refrigerator for snacks and soft drinks, and maybe even a microwave oven.

Wet-bar base cabinets are taller than normal – usually 42 inches high – to make them more convenient to use. Many cabinet manufacturers offer wall cabinets with built-in wine racks or undercabinet racks for storing stemware. If you plan to include an undercounter refrigerator, be sure to check that your cabinet configuration will allow enough space for it.

Jig time

Jigs make it easy to mark the location of cabinet knobs and pulls. To mark for door hardware, slip the door jig over the corner of the door and mark through the appropriate holes. To mark drawers, pull out the drawer and mark the center of the drawer face along its upper edge. Set the drawer jig over the drawer, align the mark on the top edge of the jig with the center mark on the drawer face, and mark through the holes on the front of the jig. Both jigs have several sets of holes so you can mark for different-sized hardware – be sure to use the right holes.

Fill any gaps between the hanging rail and the wall with shims so the cabinet won't rack out of square when you screw the cabinet to the wall. Remember to screw through the shims.

To mark the sink opening in a plastic laminate countertop, use the manufacturer's sink template. A particleboard brace across the opening keeps the waste piece from breaking off and chipping the laminate.

Matching filler strips on each side of the cabinet make it fit snug to the walls. Scribe the filler strips to the wall, then attach them to the cabinet. Place the screws so they'll be hidden by the hinges.

Set the sink in place, then attach the P-trap to the sink tailpiece and drain line trap adapter fitting. Note the GFCI receptacle – a requirement any time you install an outlet near water. Provide enough receptacles for a refrigerator, blender, undercabinet lights, and other electrical amenities.

Laundry Room

Finishing a laundry room is a simple improvement that not only makes the room more pleasant to be in, but makes it more convenient to work in. Finishing the ceiling and floor makes the room easier to clean, too.

Good lighting is important in a laundry room. In this laundry room, one recessed fluorescent light is located over the work area, and another is over the washer and dryer. The addition of base cabinets and a countertop creates a useful workstation. Upper cabinets, shelves, and drawers provide additional storage.

A built-in ironing board is a great convenience in a laundry room, especially if it has multiple height settings. (Typically, a height of 32 to 36 inches off the floor is considered ergonomically correct, depending on the height of the individual doing the ironing.) Make sure to wire for task lighting above the ironing board – an outlet with a timer for the iron is another nice touch. In this case, non-metallic sheathed cable runs above the suspended ceiling and is pulled through the ironing board's junction box.

To install base cabinets, shim the first cabinet plumb and level then screw it to the wall. Align the second cabinet to the first, shim it level and plumb, then clamp the cabinets together. Screw them together through the face frames before screwing the second cabinet to the wall.

Apply glue to the top of the cabinets, center the countertop, and fasten it to the cabinets by screwing up through the corner blocks. The strips attached to the cabinet edges compensate for the buildup on the front edge of the countertop; without them, the counter would sit an inch lower and interfere with the drawers.

Feed the cable into the ironing board's junction box as you set the unit in place. The ironing board fits in a standard stud cavity.

The middle base cabinet has a convenient built-in laundry basket.

Home Theater

Before ordering any cabinets, get the dimensions of the television, speakers, and other electronic equipment you'll be installing. Standard cabinets are 24 inches deep and may not accommodate a large TV unless it sticks out in front. To set the TV farther in, you can cut an opening in the cabinet back and then either build the entertainment center across a corner, or stagger the placement of the cabinets so that the TV cabinet sits forward of the ones on both sides.

Speaker wire can be tricky to run just because you may not be sure where you want to locate the speakers at the time you do the rough-ins. Our solution is to pick the general

To pull two runs of coaxial cable at once, reel out the cable required for both runs, loop it in half, then pull the loop to the boxes and cut it. When you cut the loop you have two runs of cable. Leave 6 to 8 inches of excess cable in each box for doing hookups.

Weave speaker cable back and forth in the joist cavity in the general area where the speaker will be located and loosely tack it up with electrical staples. Then, you can pull down as much as you need when you install the speakers.

vicinity for the speaker and string speaker cable back and forth across that joist cavity, lightly tacking it to the joists. Then, when you're ready to install the speakers, you cut holes for the speakers and reach up into the ceiling to pull down some speaker wire. A couple of quick tugs should free the cable from the staples you used to tack it up there.

We prefer to home-run coaxial cable. That way we can install a distribution amplifier if one is needed. You do have to pull a lot more cable to do this, however. One trick we use is to locate the boxes for adjoining rooms in the same stud cavity. Then we reel out the approximate amount of cable needed to reach that location and back, loop it in half, and pull the looped cable to the boxes. Snip the loop and you have two cable runs with only one cable pull.

To hide speakers, order the cabinet doors without panels and staple fabric over the openings.

Index